CONTENTS

FIND YOUR ADVENTURE!

Fortrose
Dingwall
A835
Nairn
A9
A96
Ross-shire
Nairnshire & Moray
Inverness
Loch Ness
Inverness-shire
A9
Aviemore
A82
Cairngorms National Park

Wee Adventure together!

We asked families, **'What makes a walk fun for kids and adults?'**
They said: **adventure challenge play learning bike**
paddling easy to find all weather play parks pram
We think this book has it covered. Enjoy your ad

LIFE WAS MEANT FOR G
FRIENDS & GREAT ADVEN

3

INTRODUCTION

This little book is all about discovering new places together, being active and loving the outdoors.

sharing our adventures

We asked local people to share their favourite places to walk and bike as a family around Inverness and up to an hour drive from the city. The result is this wonderful collection of adventures to share with you!

explore and discover

Each of the **24 adventures** has at least two routes to pick from so you will find something to suit all ages and ability. It's all free fun and most of it can be done in a pair of wellies. We have provided lots of useful information so you can plan your day out, or a short potter, based on what people big and small feel up for. Each adventure is equipped with facts and things to talk about, think about, and see on the move.

Look out for the wheel symbol, with information on routes suitable for bikes, prams, wheelchairs and scooters. Look out for the compass symbol; older children and teenagers can challenge themselves on Go Large routes too.

We know that all wee adventurers pause for a grumble sometimes, and a stop for ice cream is often as important as making that hill top.

So, don't miss the **Games for Adventurers, Inverness City Play parks** and **Foodie Adventures** at the back, to help keep feet moving and smiles on faces.

Enjoy, look after and keep sharing this amazing natural adventure playground on our doorstep.

The Wee Adventure team. **www.weeadventurescotland.co.uk**

'Take an adventure together in this beautiful area of the Highlands and Moray. On beaches, down glens, up hills, through forests, around lochs and past farmland.'

find your adventure by foot

Difficulty ratings – green boot, yellow boot, red boot
The coloured boot symbol should be matched to the terrain description and distance written next to each walk and cycle route.

Green boot – **rated easier**
Mostly flat or gentle ups and downs. Not too long (Less than 4km).

Yellow boot – **rated medium difficulty**
May include one or two steep uphill sections. Or it may be quite flat, but a bit further in distance (more than 4km).

Red boot – **rated more difficult**
Includes some steep or long uphill sections and is further in distance (more than 4km).

Note. We have not included 'time needed' to complete any walk or cycle, except in Go Large. In a family guide, it is so dependent on the age and ability of the walker or cyclist.

find your adventure by wheel

Wheel symbol
Where a walk is considered **bicycle**, **pram** or **wheelchair** friendly, it will have a wheel symbol and a description. Where there is no wheel symbol, it is probably best done on foot.

With the huge variety in models of prams and wheelchairs, they are split into off-road or standard. Bikes are split into mountain bike or standard. Please use the following descriptions for you to decide what your make or model (and the cyclist or pusher!) can handle. Sometimes only part of a route will be suitable for a pram or wheelchair, which will be made clear.

pram & wheelchair friendly routes

For the purposes of this guide:
Standard pram or wheelchair is designed to push happily on tarmac or hard packed stone paths or tracks. Boardwalks are included in this.

Off-road pram or wheelchair is designed to tackle some muddy patches and loose stone or rocky paths. These routes may need some navigation around a seasonal muddy puddle or have a narrower section of path.

bicycle friendly routes & bus info

For the purposes of this guide:
Standard bike is a bike designed for tarmac, gravel and hard packed dirt paths, the odd muddy patch and some gentler hills.

Mountain bike is a bike with gears and tyres designed for steep hills, rough muddy ground and rocky terrain.

Balance bike is a bike designed for kids age 5 and under to use on mostly flat, tarmac or hard packed surfaces. Sometimes scooters will get a mention too!

The bus symbol is used where you can reach the start point by public transport from Inverness.
www.travelinescotland.com

Wet weather symbol – indicates routes sheltered by trees.

0 mile	0.5 mile	1 mile	1.5 mile	2 mile

0 km	0.5 km	1 km	1.5 km	2 km	2.5 km	3 km

km – mile conversion

INTRODUCTION

5

River Ness Islands

INVERNESS-SHIRE & CAIRNGORMS

INVERNESS-SHIRE & CAIRNGORMS

🄻 Easy. Less than 4km
🄻 Medium. More than 4km
🄻 Difficult. More than 4km
⊗ Wheel friendly routes
🧭 Go Large. Challenging routes

Please see page 5 for more detailed information.

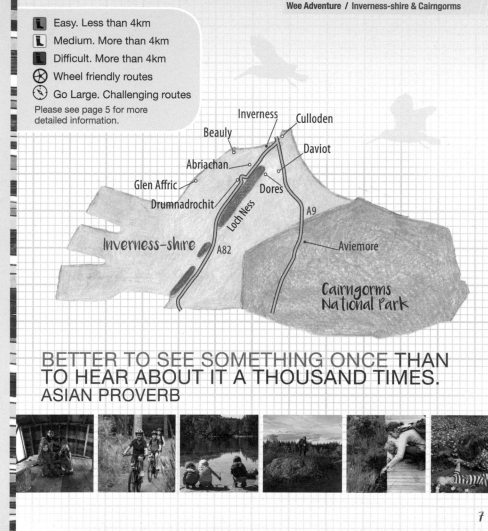

Inverness
Culloden
Beauly
Daviot
Abriachan
Glen Affric
Dores
Drumnadrochit
Loch Ness
A9
Inverness-shire
A82
Aviemore
Cairngorms National Park

BETTER TO SEE SOMETHING ONCE THAN TO HEAR ABOUT IT A THOUSAND TIMES.
ASIAN PROVERB

TREASURE ISLAND EXPLORERS, INVERNESS

This adventure is steps from Inverness city centre but instantly feels away from it all along the banks of the River Ness.

River Ness Islands, Inverness City

The islands are a maze of giant old pines, winding paths, Victorian footbridges and modern sculptures. After dark this walk is magical because it is lit up by tree lights and street lamps. You can also say you've done part of the Great Glen Way.

River Ness Islands loop ⊗

Flat, on tarmac paths. 2.8km loop. Suitable for all bikes, prams and wheelchairs. From the start point cross the footbridge over to the first island (A) (see map on page 11).

Turn right and walk to the far tip of this island to where the river diverges. You're at the top of two islands in the middle of the River Ness. Now choose whichever path you wish and meander down the two islands. The trees are great for hide and seek and there are sculpted wooden benches. The mini **stone amphitheatre** has hidden carvings.

After the third footbridge (B), turn left and keep walking with the river on your left back towards the city for about 1km.

At the end of Ladies Walk you will see the final large footbridge (C) by the War Memorial Gardens. Turn left and cross it then turn right and walk to the T junction. From here you can see **Eden Court** straight ahead of you (D), an arts hub for all ages including exhibitions, theatre and cinema. It is worth a look to see what is on, have a coffee or a full meal. The first floor is a child friendly space with a mini theatre to play in. To the right of Eden Court is **St Andrew's Cathedral**, also open to visitors.

To get back to the start point, you simply join the riverside pavement again. Don't cross the river this time but keep it on your left, walking a tree-lined route for about 1km.

(see map on page 11)

The really tall trees on the Islands are called Douglas Fir. They are around 100 years old and grow to an average of 50 metres tall.

Grey and common seals are known to come up the river as far as the bridges.

facts & tips

The City Sightseeing bus stops along this route.

extensions to this walk

This walk links with the **1500 year old city** adventure on page 12 and part of the **Caledonian Canal Adventure** on page 14.

It is an easy detour on foot to two great play parks, **Whin Park** and **Bellfield Park** (see page 96). **Inverness Botanical Gardens** (see page 93), **Inverness Leisure Centre** and the **Skate Park** are all close too. These are all marked on this map and also have their own free parking.

what it's great for

PICNIC ON BEAUTIFUL WOODEN BENCHES

PLAY HIDE & SEEK BEHIND GIANT TREES

FIND SIX BRIDGES FOR POOH STICKS

EXPLORE AN AMPHITHEATRE

FIND A PET GRAVEYARD

directions

Inverness 0.5 miles. Start from the free parking area at the **Inverness Skate Park** and **Inverness Crazy Golf** on Bught Road. Postcode area IV3 5TH. This start point is good to visit other fun spots without getting back in the car (see map and extensions to this walk).

This is a loop walk and easy to join at any point along the river from the city centre.

Treasure Island Explorers

map on following page

You'll be walking or cycling part of the **Great Glen Way**, a foot and cycle path that runs 79 miles between Inverness Castle and Fort William!

RIVER NESS ISLANDS

Furthest distance from Inverness 0.8km / 0.5miles

walk options

Loop 2.8km

9

" TREASURE ISLAND
EXPLORERS
River Ness, Eden Court & Cathedral.

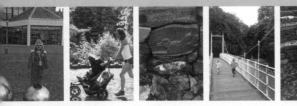

Forty Forty
Hide and Seek with a twist!

One person is a guard and the rest are raiders.

The guard chooses a base to count from, like a tree stump. All the raiders hide while the guard counts slowly to 40.

The guard must then leave base and go looking for the raiders. When a raider sees their chance, they run from their hiding place to try to reach base before the guard can get back to it.

If the guard makes it back first they shout **'Forty Forty see Jim!'** If the raider beats the guard to base they shout **'Forty Forty I'm in!'**

This continues until each raider is out of hiding. The first raider to be beaten back to base is the next guard.

10

Canal Park

Bught Road

Bught Lane

Whin Park

Bught Drive

START

Bught Road

Drummond Crescent

200m

How many sculpted benches have you seen?

Treasure Island Explorers

follow the map and find your adventure!

★ 1. Inverness Botanical Gardens
2. Inverness Leisure Centre
3. Inverness Ice Centre
4. Inverness Skate Park
5. Inverness Crazy Golf
6. Whin Park
7. Eden Court
8. St Andrew's Cathedral
9. Bellfield Park
10. Royal Northern Infirmary

amenities

(bike hire Bellfield Park) (available at Whin & Bellfield Park) (www.city-sightseeing.com)

Look out for us along the River Ness!

Dipper

Otter

Grey heron

RIVER NESS ISLANDS
Furthest distance from Inverness 0.8km / 0.5miles

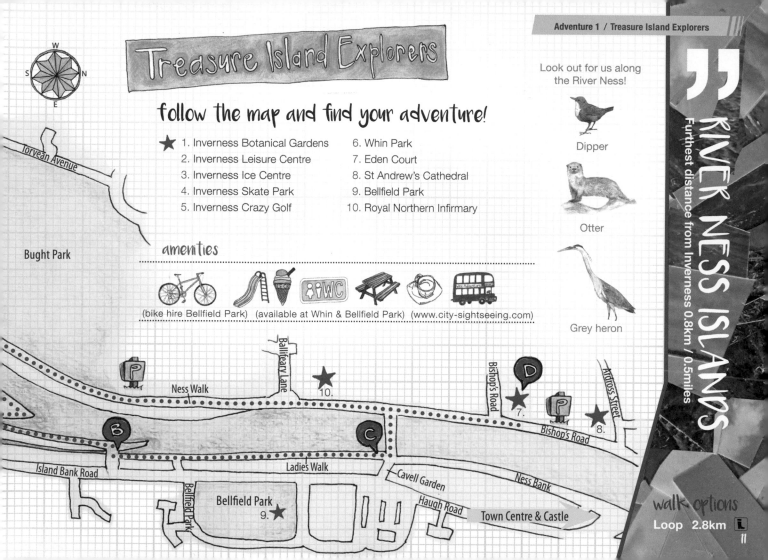

Torvean Avenue

Bught Park

Ness Walk

Ballifeary Lane

10.

Bishop's Road

D

7.

Ardross Street

Bishop's Road

8.

Island Bank Road

Ladies Walk

Cavell Garden

Ness Bank

Bellfield Park

Haugh Road

Town Centre & Castle

Bellfield Park
9. ★

walk options

Loop 2.8km

11

1500 YEAR OLD CITY, INVERNESS

Take an easy walk around the centre of Inverness to discover these little snippets of history.

Starting at Inverness Castle

Even though the Picts were the first people known to have settled in Inverness by the 6th century AD, the first castle on this site wasn't built until 1057. Since then there has been plenty of bloody conflict. This castle is quite modern, built in 1836. The previous one was blown up after the Battle of Culloden. **Inverness Museum & Art Gallery** (free) and the **VisitScotland tourist information centre** are located behind the castle.

Hold on! Standing in front of the castle or up in the **Inverness Castle Viewpoint** (charge), look down to the River Ness and left up the Great Glen towards Loch Ness. Inverness sits on the Great Glen Fault, meaning there is a small earthquake risk. The last one was recorded in 1934.

history

How rude! Mary Queen of Scots visited Inverness in 1562. She wanted to stay in the castle but got turned away. A bad decision, because the governor responsible was later hanged.

enjoy the view

Head down Castle Street to Inverness Town House.
This Victorian Gothic building is the site of the only meeting of the British Government ever held outside England. **Why here?** In 1921 the Prime Minister was holidaying in the Highlands when the Republic of Ireland declared it wanted to break away from the United Kingdom. So, he brought the Cabinet up to him rather than going back to London for a meeting!

Meander down Church Street.
Pedestrian opening opposite Inverness **Town House**. Discover the oldest house in Inverness, Abertarff House, the largest second hand book shop in Scotland, Leakey's Book Shop, and The Old High Church graveyard with a gruesome history. After the 1746 Battle of Culloden, Jacobite prisoners were executed in this graveyard. There is a historical information board in the graveyard.

Yum! Perfect homemade ice cream can be found at **Miele's Gelateria Inverness**.

Nearby, **The Victorian Market** is under cover and nice to wander around. **Elementary my dear Watson.** The original

Sherlock Holmes from Victorian times famously wears a large overcoat called an Inverness Cape. Can't think why a garment designed for rain might have originated here!?

Head up the High Street towards the Crown area.
Venture to the top of the pedestrian High Street. Across from the Eastgate centre entrance, go up Stephen's Brae to the Crown area. Go past **Velocity Café and Bicycle Workshop** (great coffee). The Crown is an example of Inverness's prosperity in Victorian times, with big hotels and some grand houses. **Walker Park play park** is in Crown too, on Kingsmills Road (see page 96).

walk or cycle ⊗

Enjoy kilometres of tarmac pathways on either side of the River Ness towards Inverness Port. There are sculptures and seating along the way. The river has been an international port for 100's of years; trading fish, fur, wool, rope and currently wind turbines. A detailed information board of routes can be found by the river, on the cathedral side of the bridge.

Falcon Square has a statue of a unicorn, the official animal of Scotland. The unicorn is thought to have been chosen in the late 1300's as the only match for the English lion!

INVERNESS CITY

CALEDONIAN CANAL

The canal is a unique piece of Victorian engineering, running for 60 miles (96km) from Inverness to Fort William.

the Canal

This adventure takes you along a 7 mile stretch of canal with the chance to walk over a sea lock, enter a city nature reserve, race a passing boat, learn about the mysterious hill of the yew trees or just picnic in great scenery.

a cycle along history

A third of the canal is manmade and the rest is made up of four lochs, **Loch Dochfour, Loch Ness, Loch Oich** and **Loch Lochy**. The canal took 12 years to build, starting in 1803. One purpose was to provide employment to local Highlanders because the devastation of the Highland Clearances meant many locals were emigrating overseas or south. The other was to create a much calmer route for wooden boats to move from the east to west coast, without having to tackle the perilous North Sea around the tip of

Scotland. However, by the time the canal was built, it wasn't deep or wide enough for many modern steel ships to use it!

Building the canal did provide 3000 jobs (and more to this day) and a safe route to use in the First World War so some ships could avoid the danger of enemy presence around the North Coast. Queen Victoria took a trip along it in 1873 and it began life as a fashionable tourist attraction.

Clachnaharry [Inverness] to Dochgarroch village 11km/7 miles one way.

This canal path adventure can be done as one ambitious big loop, or in smaller sections. Three start points along the canal are suggested (see map), all with free parking and smaller walks or cycles close by if you don't fancy the entire route. Match the stars on the map to the sites of interest near each start point and explore the scenery and amazing engineering of this unique waterway.

enjoy the ride

All the tow paths are hard packed gravel or tarmac (some pot holes) and suitable for all types of bike, pram and most wheelchair users.

start point A. Clachnaharry

Clachnaharry used to be a small fishing village but it has now merged with Inverness city. The sea lock marks the start of the eastern end of the Caledonian Canal, where it connects with the Beauly Firth. A railway swing bridge also crosses the canal at Clachnaharry, taking trains up the Far North Line to Thurso and Wick.

⭐ **Walk 1. Short loop of the sea lock. Flat, 1km loop.** To experience the very tip of the Caledonian Canal, walk or cycle this part of the tow path, built out into the Beauly Firth, and cross over the footbridge at the sea lock to return back on the other side. A footpath crosses the railway line by the white wooden signal box. Take care!

⭐ **Walk 2. Merkinch Local Nature Reserve. Flat, 1.2km loop.** This signed trail is a small detour off the canal path at the Clachnaharry end. The nature reserve is full of wildlife including wading birds, cormorants, herons, owls, weasels and roe deer. You may even spot kingfishers and the occasional osprey. It takes you alongside salt water tidal pools, fresh water ponds and the Beauly Firth with great views over to the Black Isle and the Kessock Bridge. This is the best city spot to see dolphins at high tide.

Follow the trail along the sea wall to the old ticket office and ferry port, where ferries used to go back and forth to North Kessock before the bridge was built in 1982. Turn back on yourself and take the left-hand path to loop back to the canal.

Merkinch P.S.

⭐ **Good to see! Muirtown Four Locks and Muirtown Basin.** Muirtown Basin is a marina, built to be a second port for Inverness in the 1800's, but never needed. The path crossing the busy A862 by the canal swing bridge leads up to Muirtown Locks. A flight of four locks, this allows boats to travel up or down hill!

directions to start point A. 🚗

Inverness centre 1.3 miles. Take the A862 towards Beauly. There is limited roadside parking around Clachnaharry. Or, turn right off Telford Street directly before the Muirtown Locks road bridge for parking by the marina. Postcode area IV3 5LE.

what it's great for

WATCH HOW A CANAL LOCK WORKS

CYCLE ALONG FLAT TOW PATHS

EXPLORE A CITY NATURE RESERVE

VIEW SCOTTISH ENGINEERING HISTORY

CLIMB A CEMETERY HILL

CALEDONIAN CANAL
Furthest distance from Inverness up to 8km / 5miles

walk options
Walk 1. 1km 🇮
Walk 2. 1.2km 🇱

15

CALEDONIAN CANAL

The canal was constructed by Scottish engineer Thomas Telford who made a lasting impression on his native Scotland, and far beyond.

start point B. Whin Park

Along the tow path from Whin Park, Clachnaharry is 3.7km and Dochgarroch is 5.8km one way. Whin Park is a huge play park with a boating pond and miniature railway to ride on (seasonal).

⭐ **Walk 3. River Ness Islands. Flat, on tarmac. 3.2km loop.** Take a short detour from Whin Park on foot or bike along the River Ness Islands to the city centre. See the map on page 11.

⭐ **Walk 4. Tomnahurich Hill and cemetery. Steady incline on tarmac and track. 2km return.** Tomnahurich Hill, meaning hill of the yew trees, has graves dating back to the 1800's and is still a city cemetery. Paths lead up

Tomnahurich Hill folklore. One night, a travelling fiddler fell asleep on the hill and woke up in an underworld palace. He is made to play all night for the entertainment of the fairy queen at a great fairy feast. He finally awoke on the shores of the River Ness, only to discover that 200 years had passed and he crumbled to dust.

the hill through trees to a war memorial at the top. The hill is an esker mound, left over from the Ice Age.

amenities

Cafés in Inverness Botanic Garden and Inverness Leisure Centre (all year). Public toilets and refreshment kiosk at Whin Park (seasonal).

directions to start point B.

Inverness centre 1 mile. Free parking at Whin Park, Bught Road. Postcode area IV3 5SS.

Look out for us along Merkinch Nature Reserve!

Osprey

Cormorant

Kingfisher

16

EVERY MOMENT IS A FRESH BEGINNING. T.S. ELIOT

1km

Beauly Firth

Beauly

A862

railway line

Clachnaharry

Inverness

swing bridge

A862

Bught Rd

Caledonian Canal

Bught Park

A82

swing bridge

A82

Fort William

A82

WhinPark

STARR B

P

START C

school

P

5.

Dochgarroch

B862

© Crown copyright 2017 Ordnance Survey 100058484

big kids
Kayak to Loch Ness along the Caledonia Canal!

start point C. Dochgarroch Lock

Dochgarroch village is a pretty place to sit on the canal banks, have a picnic and watch the boats go through a single lock. **Fact.** A canal lock works by raising and lowering water levels, to allow boats to cross over land that is not level.

⭐ **Walk 5. Canal and River Ness merge point. Flat, 1km loop.** Where the canal and River Ness converge at a weir, boats begin their journey on the first eastern end loch, Loch Dochfour. This turns into Loch Ness after only 1 mile. From the village, cross the footbridge over the canal lock and turn right along the grass canal path. Walk all the way to the end and loop left around the top of this little peninsula in the middle of the canal and the River Ness. Walk back along the riverside path, taking the first left path to get back to the canal path (the path along the river side is uneven and not wheelchair or pram friendly).

amenities

Public toilets and picnic tables. Seasonal restaurant.

directions to start point C.

Inverness centre 5 miles. Take the A82 out of Inverness towards Fort William. Free parking in village. Postcode area IV3 8JG.

CALEDONIAN CANAL
Furthest distance from Inverness up to 8km / 5miles

walk options

Walk 3. 3.2km
Walk 4. 2km
Walk 5. 1km

ICE AGE TRAIL, NEAR DAVIOT

This fun little walk was shaped by glaciers in the last Ice Age and, despite being mostly on the flat, it provides plenty of views and adventure through woods and heather, along esker ridges and past kettlehole lochans.

snow tip

In winter, this is a great place to go for a snow walk. Snow often lies here even when it hasn't in Inverness. The lochan looks magical frozen over.

facts

Quick geography lesson. Esker ridges are sometimes confused with railway embankments but they were formed by nature over 13 thousand years ago! The esker is made up of sand and gravel left behind by a river that once flowed inside the ice-walled tunnel of a huge glacier. The glacier ran all the way down the Great Glen and eventually melted away to leave the ridges jutting out.

WE DIDN'T REALISE WE WERE MAKING MEMORIES. WE JUST KNEW WE WERE HAVING FUN. A. A. MILNE / WINNIE THE POOH

18

Littlemill, near Daviot

Something about this walk encourages adventurers big and small to run ahead and explore. It might be the satisfying winding trails and changing landscape to discover around each corner.

This walk is great for wildlife; spot deer, listen out for cuckoos and watch your feet for frogs! The area is a Site of Special Scientific Interest. Forestry Commission Scotland has set up three signed trails, red, blue and yellow with information signs along the way.

walk 1. Esker Trail

Slight inclines and some narrow paths. 2.6km loop (red trail). This trail is a good example of the glacial landscape, including lochans and esker ridges.

walk 2. all three trails

Slight inclines and some narrow paths. 5km loop (blue, red and yellow trails combined). This is a great longer option and includes the quarry pond, a longer ridge section and flat forestry tracks. Start on the blue trail going anti-clockwise, then red, then end on yellow.

amenities

There are no amenities by this walk. However, nearby **The Dairy at Daviot** makes and sells beautiful Black Isle Dairy ice cream in any flavour you can imagine. There is also a family restaurant, play park and small nature trail. On the A9 towards Perth, look for the black and white cow sign to Daviot Dairy on your left, about 3 miles out of Inverness (also signed to Croy). Still on the A9, just past the Dairy turning, is **Daviot Antiques**, a friendly treasure trove of old intriguing items for sale set up in the garden and outhouses. Kids find it fascinating (but keep a close eye on them!).

directions

Inverness 8 miles. Take the A9 towards Perth. After 5 miles take the right hand turn onto the B851 signed to Fort Augustus. 1.5 miles down this road you will see green Forestry Commission signs for Littlemill on the left. The free parking area at the start of the walk is on the left by a metal gate. There is an information board with a map at the start. Postcode area IV2 6WG.

what it's great for

SEE A LANDSCAPE SHAPED BY GLACIERS

FIND THE PERFECT PADDLING STREAM

SPOT ROE DEER

PICNIC BY A LOCHAN EDGE

RUN ALONG A HEATHERY RIDGE

LITTLEMILL

Furthest distance from Inverness 13km / 8miles

walk options

Walk 1. 2.6km
Walk 2. 5km

BATTLEFIELD ADVENTURE, CULLODEN

Explore 4000 years of history on this collection of excellent things to do with the family in the Culloden area, on foot or wheels.

Culloden

The Battle of Culloden forms a huge part of the history of Scotland. But, who'd have known the Culloden area also has prehistoric tombs to huddle in, a Victorian viaduct, a Cloutie well and life size Gruffalo characters to find in the woods?

Bite size history. The Battle of Culloden in 1746 was the last major battle fought on British soil. Clans from all over the Highlands joined the Jacobites, led by Bonnie Prince Charlie, to fight against British Government forces including Scottish lowlanders. The Jacobites were normal Highlanders who wanted control over their own land and way of life, and Bonnie Prince Charlie wanted to be King. The fighting lasted only one hour. The Jacobites were thwarted by poor planning, inferior numbers of men, weapons and lack of food. Many met a horrible death as prisoners of war. Gaelic culture in the Highlands was crushed for many decades.

walk 1. Culloden Battlefield ⊗

Flat, tarmac and hard packed gravel paths. 2km loop. Standard pram, wheelchair and bike friendly. Culloden battlefield is free and accessible for everyone to walk or cycle on. Today, the moor still has a wild and desolate feel. Flags show the battle lines and stones mark the graves of fallen clansmen. Information boards around the route tell the full story of the battle. You can go as little or as far as you like, the atmosphere will capture you. They say that since the battle, the birds don't sing here, can you hear any?

Step back in time. Stand on the moor and imagine how it felt to line up for battle here on a bleak day in April; rain and sleet driving at you, the roar of men and heavy guns around you and unending bog and thickets to cross.

walk 2. Battlefield Trail ⊗

Flat with some inclines, one steep section. All on firm tracks and cycleways. 9.6km/6 mile loop. Standard bike, off-road pram and wheelchair friendly. This trail is waymarked by wooden sign posts. Two short sections run on roadside footpaths, otherwise it is completely clear of roads. It goes through Culloden Wood, over the battlefield and past farmland. Along the way, significant points in the history of battle such as the **Prisoner's Stone**, **Cumberland's Stone** and **The Well of the Dead** are signed.

Cycle route extension. 4.8km loop. Clava Cairns and **Culloden Viaduct** (walks 5 and 6) can be done by bike as a detour extension to the Culloden Battlefield Trail, for those confident to ride on minor roads. Look for the right hand turn after passing the Culloden Battlefield Visitor Centre.

amenities

The Culloden Battlefield Visitor Centre Exhibition is excellent (entrance charge, or free to National Trust for Scotland members and 5 year olds and under). The battlefield, café and toilets are open to everyone without having to pay any entrance charge. www.nts.org.uk/culloden See the Foodie Adventure on page 92 for the nearby **Cantray Park** amenities too.

directions to walk 1. & 2.

Inverness 5.5 miles. Take the B9006 out of Inverness, signed to Culloden Moor and Croy. Two miles after the 40mph signs end, the battlefield flags are clear and visitor centre is signed on the right. Park in the Culloden Battlefield and Visitor Centre car park (charge), or there are a few free parking spaces before the barrier to the visitor centre. Postcode IV2 5EU.

what its great for

IMAGINE BEING A JACOBITE IN BATTLE

CYCLE THROUGH THE HISTORY OF CULLODEN

STAND UNDER A HUGE RAILWAY VIADUCT

WALK INTO A BRONZE AGE TOMB

FIND A LIFE SIZE GRUFFALO

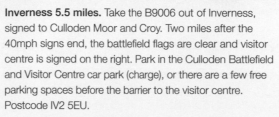

CULLODEN
Furthest distance from Inverness 10km / 6.5miles

FULL OF GRIEF, THE LOW WINDS SWEEP, O'ER THE SORROW-HAUNTED GROUND... ALICE MACDONELL LATE 1800'S

walk options
Walk 1. 2km
Walk 2. 9.6km

walk 3. Culloden Woods trail ⊗

Some inclines, 2.4km loop. Standard bike, off-road prams and wheelchairs. Culloden Wood, on the edge of Inverness city, is a sheltered walk all year-round. A Forestry Commission Scotland information board in the car park details the **yellow trail** through pine woodland; past the **Cloutie Well** and the **Prisoner's Stone**, alongside streams and over a railway line. You can start the **Culloden Battlefield Trail** (walk 2) from here too.

Folklore of a Cloutie well. On the Culloden Battlefield trail and Culloden Wood trail you pass St Mary's Well in Culloden Wood, a Cloutie well. Clout is another word for rag, or cloth. Starting over 2000 years ago, people dipped a piece of cloth in the spring waters of the well and used it to rub on an ailment or worry, then tie to a tree. It was believed this would heal, protect and keep away evil spirits. St Mary's Well is still used today.

for small wheels ⊗

The Inverness Campus of the university (UHI) is popular at the weekend with younger children gaining confidence at cycling or scootering. There are plenty of safe, wide, flat footpaths through large landscaped grounds, around a small lochan. There are some fun sculptures to go over too. The campus is 1.5 miles from Inverness. Take the B9006 from Inverness towards Culloden and Croy, then follow the signs in to the distinctive campus on the left. Designated free parking.

amenities 👜 ♿WC

Follow your nose to **Harry Gow's bakery**, it's 250m further down Tower Road and turn right into Smithton Industrial Estate. The family friendly **Kings Factory Café** is also next door (best bacon rolls and often has a play area open for younger children). **Simpson's Garden Centre**, 2 miles back towards Inverness off the B9006 is very good.

directions to walk 3. 🚗

Inverness 4 miles. Follow the B9006 to Culloden and Croy. After 2 miles, turn left onto Tower Road signed for Smithton, Culloden, Balloch. After 1 mile, turn right into the free Forestry Commission Scotland signed car park. Postcode area IV2 7LT.

'Do you think it feels a relaxing place, or a little eerie at St Mary's Well?'

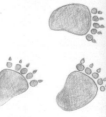

walk 4. The Gruffalo Walk and Culloden House ⊗

Flat, on tarmac and away from roads. 1.5km return. Standard bike, pram and wheelchair friendly. Great for scooters too! Wooden sculptures of giant children's book characters make an appearance along a tree lined walkway, starting from Tower Road in Smithon and ending at Culloden House Hotel grounds. **Meet a dragon, a wizard, the Gruffalo, his 'friends', and more.**

At **Culloden House** (now a luxury hotel), you are welcome to walk the grounds. There's a duck pond just to the right after the entrance gates and a beautiful walled garden (ask for key at reception). In the run-up to the Battle of Culloden in 1746, Bonnie Prince Charlie used this house as his battle headquarters.

directions to walk 4. 🚗

Inverness 4 miles. See directions for Culloden Woods, walk 3. Park in the Culloden Wood car park and walk downhill by pavement on Tower Road for 200m. The black gates signed Culloden Avenue are on your right by the traffic lights. Or, park in the Smithton Industrial Estate. Walk out of the entrance, turn left and the black gates are on your left after 50m. Postcode IV2 7WL.

I OPENED A BOOK AND IN I STRODE. NOW NOBODY CAN FIND ME. JULIA DONALDSON

CULLODEN
Furthest distance from Inverness 10km / 6.5miles

walk options
Walk 3. 2.4km
Walk 4. 1.5km

BATTLEFIELD ADVENTURE, CULLODEN

Farmland all over the Highlands is dotted with stone circles and structures, showing signs of our prehistoric predecessors.

step back in time

walk 5. Clava Cairns Bronze Age Site

Flat, 400m loop. Clava Cairns are tucked away in a beautiful spot, not far in distance from Culloden Battlefield but 4000 years away in time! This is a **Bronze Age cemetery** with over 20 prehistoric structures that have been really well preserved. Nobody really knows for sure exactly what each tomb was designed for but the site was probably used for burials over a time period of 1000 years. We also know they were cleverly built to allow sunlight on the shortest and longest days of the year (winter and summer solstice) to shine directly onto sacred parts of the tombs.

directions to walk 5.

Inverness 6.5 miles. Take the B9006 from Inverness. Just past the entrance to Culloden Battlefield Visitor Centre, take the right turn signed to Clava Cairns 1.5 miles, and follow the signs in. Free to enter all year, car park at the site. Postcode area IV2 5EU.

walk 6. Culloden Viaduct

Flat, uneven ground. Path sometimes narrow, uneven and close to river edge. 1km return. Stand directly beneath a hugely impressive piece of Victorian architecture, built in 1898. **It's the longest railway viaduct in Scotland and is still used by trains today.** This short walk uses grass tracks by the banks of the River Nairn. From the parking spot, walk down the road 20m and cross a stile by a metal gate on the corner. Take the left fork on a rough grassy path and aim for the viaduct. It joins the riverside footpath after about 800m, turn left to stand under the viaduct beside the river. Option to return directly along the river bank.

Viaduct; Latin 'via', for road and 'ducere', to lead.

directions to walk 6.

About 1 mile before the Clava Cairns (see Walk 5), coming down the hill, just before you cross the road bridge over the River Nairn, there is a small layby on your right. Park here. **Alternatively**, you can continue along the road and instead of turning right to the cairns, keep straight on and drive (cycle or walk) under the other end of the viaduct on tarmac road.

Feel the history. Walk into the largest tomb, huddle down and imagine who built this. What were they wearing, what did they have to worry about, what did they do for fun?

CULLODEN

Furthest distance from Inverness 10km / 6.5miles

W N S E

1km

Moray Firth

railway line

Aberdeen/Nairn

A96

Culloden House Hotel

Culloden

Balloch

railway line

A96

Harry Gow Industrial Estate

Croy

2

2,3,4

Culloden Wood

Viaduct

Inverness Campus UHI

Cradlehall

Tower Rd

B9006

1,2

6

Clava Cairns

Culloden Battlefield

5

A9

Inverness

Inshes roundabout

Westhill

B9006

A9

River Nairn

© Crown copyright 2017 Ordnance Survey 100058484

walk options

Walk 5. 400m

Walk 6. 1km

25

"THE NESSIE HUNTER, LOCH NESS

Try to track down the Loch Ness Monster on this adventure which takes you right along the pebbled shores of Loch Ness and into the woods.

Loch Ness, Dores

Standing on Dores beach, you are looking down the Great Glen towards Fort William and the west coast. The Caledonian Canal joins up four lochs; Loch Lochy, Loch Oich, Loch Ness and Loch Dochfour. This makes one continuous body of water so people can travel all the way from the Highland's east to west coast by water.

> For shorter legs. These two larger loops can easily be made into shorter loops to suit the mood on the day. See the map for suggested short cuts.

walk 1. Dores Beach & Torr Wood

Mostly flat, one uphill section. 5.5km loop (red route on map). You can make the red loop much shorter by taking one of the suggested short cuts (see map). Starting from the Dores Inn car park, walk along the beach, or the grass path behind the beach for about 400m. The grass path leads to a metal gate into Torr Wood (A) (cut up to the grass path towards the end of the beach if you walk along the stones to find this point). Take the path that forks first right gently uphill for about 50 metres. At a T junction, turn right onto the path that leads under pines and over their giant roots, then into open beech wood. Follow it round until it reaches a junction with a grass vehicle track (B). Turn right and continue along the track for about 1km where it ends at another junction with a gravel vehicle track by a high wooden gate (C). Turn left to walk downhill, eventually passing a cream cottage on your right. At the bottom there is a jetty, boat mooring point and smaller sheltered pebble beaches to explore.

This is all part of the Aldourie Castle Estate. The 16th century castle is in private grounds but if you're curious you can have a peek at it by taking a little diversion from the jetty area (yellow route on map, 1.5km return). Go through the small gate below the cream cottage and follow the loch side path until you see the castle (D). Then return to the jetty.

To return back to Dores take the track alongside the jetty with the water on your right, through a gate and then all the way back to the metal gate at the start of Dores beach (A). Or, for added adventure value, go down to the water's edge at (E), then follow the small track that winds tightly through the trees and will also bring you back to Dores beach.

Loch Ness has more water in it than all the lakes in England and Wales put together. At its deepest point, it is the height of 51 double decker buses deep! Because it is so deep, the water stays at a fairly constant (chilly) temperature all year around. Perfect living conditions for the Loch Ness Monster….

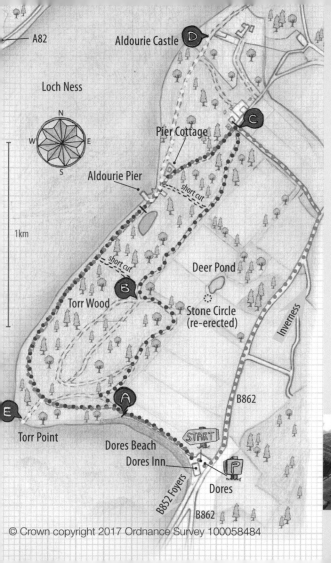

Route tip. If it's windy on Dores beach, you will be surprised at how sheltered it feels as soon as you get into the woods, so don't be put off by a westerly wind howling down the glen!

⚙ **Wheelchair access.** There is a concrete jetty down to the loch from the Dores Inn car park, so anyone can get right up close to Loch Ness and the beautiful views here. The path along the back of the beach to A, may also be suitable.

Cool fact. From Dores you can see the highest point above Loch Ness called Meall Fuar-mhonaidh. You can climb it as a Go Large adventure on page 84.

Poetic waterfalls

Keep going to **The Falls of Foyers**, a 62m high waterfall above Loch Ness, with viewpoints and fun trails (some on steep slopes). Find the red squirrel discovery trail and Robert Burns poetry engraved in rock. **Amenities.** Good play park, shop and café in village. The Camerons Tea Room and Farm Shop about 0.5 miles further down the hill is a lovely spot. **Directions.** Continue 11 miles along the B852 from Dores to Foyers village. Free parking.

LOCH NESS

Furthest distance from Inverness 13km / 8miles

walk options

Walk 1. 5.5km

27

THE NESSIE HUNTER, LOCH NESS

Some hardy locals swim in Loch Ness every month of the year. You may be tempted too on a calm, warm day. Give it a go (or at least paddle)!

THE EARTH HAS MUSIC FOR THOSE WHO LISTEN. WILLIAM SHAKESPEARE

walk 2. alternative loop ⊗

Mostly flat, one moderate uphill section. 6km loop (blue route on map). **Suitable for standard bikes, off-road prams and off-road wheelchairs.** All on paths and one short section of quiet, single track estate road, but be prepared to navigate a couple of muddy patches after rain.

From the start, take the path that runs behind Dores beach to (A). After the gate, take the lower, left hand track through the woods, and keep going straight to (C). Go through the high wooden gate onto the single tarmac road and turn immediately right, then straight on through another high gate. The estate road leads to the B862. Cross the B862 to join the tarmac footpath/cycle way, turn right and let it take you all the way back into Dores.

It is popular to cycle from Inverness to Dores. Flat, some inclines, 14km/9 miles one way.

For further information visit cycleroutes.transitionblackisle.org to use residential streets and minor roads to exit Inverness and join the B862 cyclepath.

Julie Macrae

amenities

The Dores Inn pub has public toilets and is a popular spot for a drink, coffee and cake or full meals. There is plenty of outdoor seating and free parking (it can get very busy in summer). There is a football pitch and small play park behind the car park.

directions

Inverness 8 miles. From Inverness take the B862 signed to Dores and Foyers. Stay on this road for 8 miles until you reach Dores. There is a sign for 'Free Parking 80yds,' on your entrance to the village. Officially you must be a patron of the Dores Inn to use their free car park. There is free roadside parking in the village. Postcode area IV2 6TR.

what it's great for

BE BLOWN AWAY BY THE GREAT GLEN VIEW

SKIM PEBBLES FROM A SWEEPING BEACH

GET CREATIVE WITH DRIFT WOOD

EXPLORE WOODLAND TRAILS

TRY WILD SWIMMING

Amazing! By 10 weeks old, young squirrels are ready to survive alone and leave the drey (nest). It takes most humans 18 years!

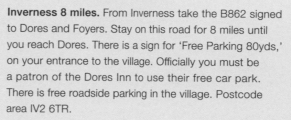

"

LOCH NESS

Furthest distance from Inverness: 13km / 8miles

walk options
Walk 2. 6km

"TREEHOUSE FUN, ABRIACHAN

A natural adventure playground in woodland and hills above Loch Ness.

Abriachan

Discover the brilliant Abriachan Forest Trust, complete with great wooden play equipment, treehouses and a boardwalk trail to a bird hide by Loch Laide. It also provides mountain bike trails and a walk up a heathery hillside to Carn Na Leitire for fantastic wild 360 degree views. Nearby, there is also a Woodland Trust trail that gives a birds-eye view of the southern end of Loch Ness.

walk 1. treehouses & bird hide ⊗

Flat 0.5km-1km loop. Standard bike, pram and wheelchair friendly. Hard packed paths and board walk. From the car park, head down the track towards the thicker pine woodland. Go straight ahead on board walks to find the bird hide overlooking Loch Laide. Or, explore left and right on the paths and find the two treehouses, camp craft areas and a small burn to paddle in (it's not a big area, you won't get lost). Keep your eyes peeled for creatures real and make believe hiding in the trees!

one minute geography lesson

Natural deforestation. Storms in 2014 and 2015 blew down a lot of the woodland here; a mixed broadleaf woodland is now regenerating, including birch, rowan, oak and aspen. In five years it will feel like a forest again. You can volunteer to help on activities that take place in this special environment. Abriachan Forest School offers lots of outdoor learning activities for all ages. www.abriachan.org.uk

walk 2. Carn Na Leitire

Some inclines with one long uphill section, 4km return.
Good hard packed paths, rocky areas. The Abriachan Forest Trust classroom has a map board beside it.

From the car park, follow the signed trail (wooden posts with birds and animals attached) that runs to the left of the **Forest Trust classroom**. Take one right fork, then at a T junction turn right. At the wooden **Round House** structure, take the left-hand path (not onto the board walk), to take you up through woodland. Out of the woods, you'll reach a fork in the path, take the fork on the left and carry on uphill. Stop on your right at the carved bench and look over the mountains to the west. Then keep going on the path you were on, diverting left, if you wish, to a celtic calendar and another view point. Then, rejoin the original path for a short walk up to the cairn at the top of **Carn Na Leitire** (434m).

mountain bike trails ✪

The trails around here are suited to family mountain biking with plenty of opportunities to test and explore. The map board by the Forest Trust classroom shows several routes of different gradings easy to difficult including a bike obstacle course, **Kelpies MTB Trail**. The easy green trail starts by following walk 2 but take the right-hand fork in the path past the woods, signed by a post with a green bike symbol. It's a one-way loop.

BELIEVE YOU CAN AND YOU'RE HALFWAY THERE.
THEODORE ROOSEVELT

ABRIACHAN
Furthest distance from Inverness 21km /13miles

what it's great for

FIND A TREEHOUSE TRAPDOOR

CLIMB TO A HILL TOP FOR 360° VIEWS

EXPLORE MOUNTAIN BIKE TRAILS

OBSERVE WILDLIFE FROM A BIRD HIDE

VIEW LOCH NESS FROM UP HIGH

walk options
Walk 1. 1km
Walk 2. 4km

31

TREEHOUSE FUN, ABRIACHAN

From high, views of Loch Ness are spectacular.

enjoy the view

walk 3. Loch Ness views

Undulating with two steep inclines. 4.2km loop. One short roadside section. On foot only.

Badger, fox and pine marten inhabit this area of woodland. It is representative of the ancient Great Glen forest where Scottish wild cat once roamed, full of hazel and oak trees. **From the car park,** take the main track uphill. After 750m, go left at a signpost to Peat

Path, Balchraggan. The narrow downhill path meets a grassy vehicle track at a T junction. Turn right. Follow this all the way, through a Woodland Trust area, to another junction with signposts and picnic tables. Take the left path downhill, signed towards Clansman and Loch Ness. The path bends left and levels out, with some rocky

areas. Where it meets a clear fork, take the left path, going uphill, then over a stile, up into Balchraggan. Follow the painted Abriachan signs. Turn right, walk down the road. At the end turn left for 200m, to the lefthand sign pointing back up the track to the Fank car park.

Nice to paddle! Loch Laide has a nice shallow entry point with a sandy bottom for paddling. There is a small layby at the side of the road by two corrugated iron boat houses.

Snow time! Abriachan gets plenty of snow in the winter and it is fun to play up here then too.

amenities

Abriachan Forest Trust has eco-friendly toilets and two BBQ areas (BYO charcoal/wood) and picnic tables.

The nearest café is the quirky **Abriachan Eco Campsite and Café**, open 365 days a year. Walk or cycle 1.5km along the **Great Glen Way** from the Forest Trust car park to reach it. Colourful signs guide the way from the gate opposite the turning into Forest Trust. It's the highest inhabited croft in Scotland; be prepared for chickens and a pig to wander past whilst you have an alfresco coffee or sandwich (and to knock on the house if you can't find anyone!).

ABRIACHAN
Furthest distance from Inverness 21km / 13miles

directions

To Abriachan Forest Trust (walks 1 and 2). Inverness 13 miles. Take the A82 to Fort William for 8.5 miles. There are two signs for Abriachan, take the second one a few miles further on from the first. Turn right up the hill and after about 2 miles take the left fork in the road, signed to **Foxhole/ Beauly and Abriachan Forest Walks**. The road now passes Loch Laide, keep going for 0.5 miles. Take the left turn at a wooden sign for Abriachan Forest Paths/Great Glen Way and the Trust area is 350m on the left.

To Loch Ness views, Balchraggan (walk 3). Inverness 11 miles. Follow the directions to Abriachan Forest Trust as far as turning off the A82. After only 1.2 miles on the uphill road, take a left turn up a stone vehicle track, with a wooden signpost to Abriachan Forest Path and Fank Parking by the track side. Park 200m further up the track (some potholes) in a parking area.

walk options
Walk 3. 4.2km

33

EXPLORE A GLEN
Explore three very different Highland glens.

the Glens

Glen Affric is a wondrous National Nature Reserve with miles of lochs, waterfalls, forest and hillside. Glen Orrin is a lesser known wilderness, great on wheels or foot, with waterfalls and a giant dam to discover. Reelig Glen is a shorter gorge walk beneath some of the tallest trees in Britain.

Glen Affric, near Cannich

Glen Affric National Nature Reserve is stunning at any time of year. The Caledonian pine forest represents what once covered most of Scotland. Wild deer, golden eagle, capercaillie, pine marten, otter and red squirrel still roam. Forestry Commission Scotland have created a number of fantastic short trails, all well maintained and clearly signed from car parks. There is no mobile phone reception in the glen.

A useful information leaflet on exploring Glen Affric can be found at www.scotland.forestry.gov.uk

walk 1. Dog Falls

Dog Falls has three trails. Undulating with some steep inclines. 1.2km-5.2km return. View the beautiful Dog Falls waterfall, walk heathery paths around Coire Loch and glimpse the islands of Loch Beinn a Mheadhain.

walk 2. Plodda Falls

Plodda Falls has two trails with some inclines. 1km or 2.4km loop. Both trails pass the waterfalls which cascade down rocks for over 40m, surrounded by mossy rocks and giant Douglas Firs. A viewing platform juts out over the waterfall.

amenities

Information point, picnic tables and toilets (Dog Falls).

directions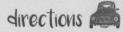

Dog Falls. Inverness 34 miles. Take the A82 to Drumnadrochit, then the A831 to Cannich. Follow signs to Glen Affric. Dog Falls car park is the first Forestry Commission car park you come to (charge). Postcode area IV4 7LZ.

Plodda Falls. Inverness 33 miles. Take the A82 to Drumnadrochit, then the A831 to Cannich. Follow signs to Tomich. Park in the free Forestry Commission Scotland Plodda Falls car park, about 3 miles past Tomich. Postcode area IV4 7LY.

 See **Go Large Inverness-shire** to tackle the amazing Glen Affric Loch Circuit (14km loop).

history

Highland Clearances and Glen Affric. Bonnie Prince Charlie hid in Glen Affric after the Battle of Culloden disaster in 1746 (see page 20). The Highland Clearances followed. In the Glen Affric area, many people were punished for supporting the Jacobite cause and removed from their small farming crofts to be replaced by mass sheep farming. This caused much damage to the natural habitat, which has now been restored over many years by conservationists.

bring binoculars

As well as the amazing views, Glen Affric's birdlife is unique. Look out for golden eagle, buzzard, osprey, crested tits, scottish crossbills and bullfinches.

Glen Orrin, near Muir of Ord

Glen Orrin takes you on a wilderness wander along the River Orrin, past waterfalls, into what feels like a forgotten glen. Take a detour to discover Loch Orrin, an impressive reservoir and appreciate it from high standing on a great dam. It's especially good for all bikes.

walk 3. Orrin Falls circuit ⊗

Mostly flat, some small inclines. The first half is a gravel vehicle track. The second half is a very quiet, tarmac minor road. 5.5km loop. First half suitable for off-road prams and wheelchairs and standard bikes. Second half suitable for all bikes, prams and most wheelchairs.

From the car park at Aultgowrie, turn right and head back down to the road you came from. Turn left and cross the River Orrin on an old stone bridge. After the bridge, turn left at the gate-house into Fairburn Estate. Follow the track along the course of the river and you will spot Orrin Falls within the first km. **There are nice spots to picnic but keep hold of smaller children near the water.** Continue to follow the track for another 1.5km. At the first junction take the left fork and at the next junction continue straight on, with the house on your right. Follow the track round to the left and cross over a bridge (an excellent one for pooh sticks!). **Can you spot any wind turbines from here?** At the green path sign for Aultgowrie 3km or Loch Orrin 5km, turn left and back down the other side of the River Orrin to Aultgowrie, this time on a good road surface. Beware, the drop down to the river on one side can be quite steep.

walk options

Walk 1. 5.2km 🅣
Walk 2. 2.4km 🅣
Walk 3. 5.5km 🅣

EXPLORE A GLEN

A strath is a large valley that is wide and shallow. A glen is typically narrower and deep.

walk 4. Loch Orrin ⊗

Loch Orrin (reservoir and dam) extension to walk 3. Tarmac, quiet, estate road, steady climb with some steep sections. 15.5 km return (10km extension to walk 3). Most bikes, prams and wheelchairs. Follow the first half of walk 3 (you can do either side of the loop depending on what surface suits you best. Turn left from the car park if you only want to use tarmac road). At the top of the loop, follow the green sign for **Loch Orrin** 5km. Continue on this road through a beautiful glen until you reach the impressive gravity dam on Loch Orrin. **Stand on top of the dam and survey your kingdom! How many wind turbines can you see?** Cross the dam, there is a smaller dam a few hundred metres further on. Return the way you came, back to the top of the circular route (walk 3). Go right to stay on tarmac to the car park, or left to use the gravelled track.

amenities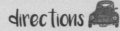

Nearby Muir of Ord (4 miles) has the popular **Bad Girl Bakery and Café** (open 7 days). Also, the **Muir Hub** is a family friendly community centre with a good cafe (open Tues-Sat).

directions 🚗

Inverness 17 miles. Take the A9 north. At the Tore roundabout take the first exit, left towards Muir of Ord. Continue through Muir of Ord, straight ahead at the crossroads and over the bridge. Take the left turn after the bridge signed towards Ullapool and Glen Ord Distillery. Turn left just before the distillery to Aultgowrie, continue for 3 miles. Once in Aultgowrie, turn left before the bridge at the green sign to Falls of Orrin circular path. There is a car park a little further up this road on your left. Postcode area IV6 7XA.

Reelig Glen, near Beauly

Reelig Glen has more trees over 60m tall than any other site in Britain. One Douglas Fir, nicknamed Dughall Mor (big dark stranger), was the tallest tree in Britain in 2000, at 64 metres high. Reelig is a steep sided river gorge with a curious stone bridge and grotto at the far end. Two waymarked **Forestry Commission Scotland** trails go through, or above, the gorge on good turf paths. Information boards in the car park and along the trails tell the story of the forest.

walk 5. Tall Trees trail

Mostly flat with one steep incline, 1.6km return. Walk along the gorge floor to the grotto and back. Paths to the picnic areas are suitable for all prams and most wheelchairs. This is a great short walk for toddlers to tackle.

walk 6. the Upper Reelig trail

Some inclines, 1.9km return. Walk up the side of the glen to explore mixed woodland on uneven paths. At the view point, can you find the stony remains of an iron-age burial site?

amenities in Beauly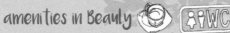

Go to Beauly (4 miles), a pretty market town, for nice cafés and fish & chips, a wander around the ancient ruin of the 13th Century **Beauly Priory** (free) and a good play park.

directions

Inverness 9.5 miles. Take the A862 to Beauly. After about 6.5 miles, turn left, signed to Moniack, Clunes and Forest Walks. Take a left fork after a long straight stretch of road and continue for another 0.5 miles. Free car park. Postcode area IV5 7PR. Buses to Moniack pass within 0.5 miles (800 metres) of Reelig Glen car park.

what its great for

FEEL A MILLION MILES AWAY
PICNIC BY RUSHING WATERFALLS
LOOK UP AT GIGANTIC NATIVE TREES
STAND ON TOP OF A GRAVITY DAM
SPOT BIRDS OF PREY

HOW DID IT GET SO LATE SO SOON? DR. SEUSS

AFFRIC, ORRIN, REELIG
Furthest distance from Inverness 54km / 34miles

walk options
Walk 4. 15.5km
Walk 5. 1.6km
Walk 6. 1.9km

CAIRNGORM LOCHS, AVIEMORE

Four magical lochs to choose from just south of Aviemore, perfect for walking, cycling or just 'being', in beautiful scenery.

Loch Morlich, Aviemore

Loch Morlich is not hidden, but it is a gem! At one end it has a huge stretch of golden sand, surrounded by mountains and a great forest for exploring the various Forestry Commission Scotland trails by foot or by bike. The beach has shade from pine trees that pop out of the sand like palm trees! Some of the trees are shaped mysteriously so are fun for climbing. The stream running onto the beach is quite shallow and fun to paddle up.

Loch Morlich is equally as stunning on a warm summer's day and a crystal cold January day when the loch often freezes over completely and will take your breath away.

walk 1. Loch Morlich trail ⊗

Flat 5.8km loop. Off-road pram, wheelchair and standard bike friendly. The full Loch Morlich loop is signed as the red trail from the car park.

walk 2. short trail ⊗

Flat 2.4km loop. Off-road pram, wheelchair and standard bike friendly. The short trail along the beach and forest behind is signed as the yellow trail from the car park.

Try The Old Logging Way. This is a safe off-road cycle path all the way from Aviemore village out to Loch Morlich, with some small hills. Approx 6km one way.

amenities

Toilets in the car park (seasonal). Snacks, ice creams and extensive watersport equipment hire and instruction is available to the public at Loch Morlich Watersports right on the beach (seasonal).

GO THE EXTRA MILE, IT'S NEVER CROWDED. AUTHOR UNKNOWN

Green Lochan [An Lochan Uaine]

Legend has it that this lochan is green because the fairies wash their clothes in it. Or, due to natural minerals in the water. It is so beautifully clear that many people paddle or swim here on a warm day. Much of the route follows a gentle river valley through gorgeous Glenmore Forest pines, as part of the Ryvoan Trail. You can choose to pick a hillier route back for amazing views and even make a short detour to a moorland bothy.

walk 3. Ryvoan trail ⊗

Mostly flat, 4km return. Standard prams, wheelchairs and bikes. This option goes out and back on the lower path of the Ryvoan Trail. It is very popular for families to walk and cycle because it is relatively flat and on wide, hard packed gravel paths.

Starting at the Glenmore Visitor Centre, take the blue trail to the right-hand side of the centre. At the junction take the right path, which leads you in front of the Reindeer Centre and up past Glenmore Lodge.

walk 4. Full Ryvoan trail

Mostly flat or down hill but with one long, uneven, steep, uphill section. 5.8km loop. Suitable on foot only. This is the full Ryvoan Trail. Start in the same direction as walk 1. At the lochan, continue to follow the trail around in a left loop along a pretty rugged trail, uphill to a view point. It then joins a long easy track downhill with great views of Loch Morlich and the CairnGorm Mountain.

walk 5. detour to a bothy ⊗

Gentle inclines, some steeper sections, 2.5km return from Green Lochan (6.5km return total). **Suitable for mountain bike only.** If you've got the energy once you reach the lochan, it's worth detouring off the blue trail and exploring the path that runs to the left and past the lochan. Quickly, the Ryvoan Pass opens up in front of you. Keep going gradually uphill, staying on the path signed to Nethy Bridge, to Ryvoan Bothy on open moorland. You can go inside for a picnic. Be aware, it can be exposed here in bad weather. Then, return the way you came.

amenities

The Glenmore Visitor Centre has an information point (including route maps) and a free exhibition about the Cairngorms by Forestry Commission Scotland.

directions

Loch Morlich Beach car park. Inverness 39 miles. Take the A9 south towards Perth. After 30 miles, take the turn off to Aviemore on the B9152. Once in Aviemore, follow signs for the CairnGorm Mountain Railway on the B970. Stay on this road for 5.5 miles. You will start to see the loch on your right and the Beach car park is signed. Small parking fee towards Forestry Commission Scotland. Postcode area PH22 1QY.

To Green Lochan parking. Inverness 39.5 miles. Follow the directions to Loch Morlich but continue along the B970 for under 0.5 miles. The Glenmore Visitor Centre car park is on the left (small charge).

AVIEMORE

Furthest distance from Inverness 64km/ 40miles

walk options

Walk 1. 5.8km
Walk 2. 2.4km
Walk 3. 4km
Walk 4. 5.8km
Walk 5. 6.5km

CAIRNGORM LOCHS, AVIEMORE

The Cairngorms National Park is the largest national park in the British Isles.

enjoy the view

Uath Lochans (Uath is pronounced 'wah')

Uath Lochans trail is special. Hidden away and quiet, it's especially beautiful in autumn. Four lochans are clustered together in Glen Feshie woodland, with some areas of bog crossed by boardwalks. It's a haven for wildlife; you can spot frogs, dragonflies and plenty of red squirrels. The more strenuous Farleitter Crag trail is fantastic for views over the Spey Valley and CairnGorm Mountain. The two trails can be combined for the more intrepid.

walk 6. Uath Lochans ⊗

Flat, some inclines 2.4km loop. Suitable for mountain bikes and off-road prams. The Uath Lochans Trail is signed as the white trail from the car park. It's an easy and interesting walk for young kids.

> **Golden eagles.** The Cairngorms National Park is one of the best places in Scotland to see a golden eagle. They have a wing span up to 2 metres!

walk 7. Farleitter Crag ⊗

Flat and undulating with one strenuous uphill section. 4km loop. Suitable for off-road prams and standard bikes. The Farleitter Crag Trail is signed as the red trail from the car park. The puff uphill is rewarded by the enchanting tall Scots pines, rocky outcrops for fabulous views and an easy route down.

amenities

Wooded picnic area and free parking.

directions

Inverness 40 miles. From Aviemore take the B9152 south for 7 miles to Kincraig. Turn left opposite the war memorial, signed to Feshiebridge. Turn right at a T-junction signed for Insh, onto the B970 (this is the same road continuing on from the directions to Loch an Eilein so it is possible to come from that direction too). Continue along the B970 for 0.5 miles. Turn left up a small winding road, marked as a no through road, for 1 mile. There is a Forestry Commission Scotland car park on your right. Postcode area PH21 1NX.

Loch an Eilein

Loch an Eilein is another great cycle loop with kids and accomplished wee balance bike adventurers should also make it round. The ruin of a small castle in the middle of a mystic loch feels very romantic and the woods surrounding the loch make for great games of imaginative play, even if you don't do the full walk and just want a perfect picnic spot.

History tip. Loch an Eilein is Gaelic for 'Loch of the Island.' The 15th century castle used to be connected to the mainland by a causeway but this is now submerged under the loch.

walk 8. Loch an Eilein ⊗

Flat 5.5km loop. A great walk or cycle that is clearly signed from the car park.

amenities 🍴 🚻WC

The Rothiemurchus Estate does charge to park cars by the loch. The Rothiemurchus Centre has a farm shop and café (off the B970).

Great cake tip! For amazing cake and the chance to spot red squirrels, pine martens, woodpeckers and many other wild birds close up as you sit in a cute tearoom, go to **The Potting Shed Tearoom at Inshriach Nursery** (March to October, closed Mon and Tue). It also has a little pond and landscaped alpine gardens to walk around. Postcode area PH22 1QS.

directions

Inverness 36 miles. Follow the directions to Loch Morlich onto the B970. At the junction by the Rothiemurchus Centre, turn right signed towards Inchriach. One mile along, take the left turn signed Loch an Eilein. Postcode area PH22 1QT.

what it's great for

SNOW-CAPPED MOUNTAINS

RURAL BEACH AWARD

CYCLE PATHS

TRYING A WATERSPORT

LOCH-SIDE FOREST WALKS

It's Snow Time! Obviously, it's wonderful to ski on the CairnGorm Mountain but if that feels a bit ambitious, go sledging by Loch Morlich instead. The Hayfields are 0.5 miles past the Glenmore Visitor Centre on the right, with parking. There are two sledging hills and a big field for snowmen and snowball fights! Check the Aviemore snow forecast. www.metoffice.gov.uk

AVIEMORE
Furthest distance from Inverness 62km / 39miles

walk options

Walk 6. 2.4km 👣
Walk 7. 4km 👣
Walk 8. 5.5km 👣

Brahan Estate

ROSS-SHIRE & BLACK ISLE

ROSS-SHIRE & BLACK ISLE

▣ Easy. Less than 4km
▣ Medium. More than 4km
▣ Difficult. More than 4km
⊗ Wheel friendly routes
⊘ Go Large. Challenging routes

Please see page 5 for more detailed information.

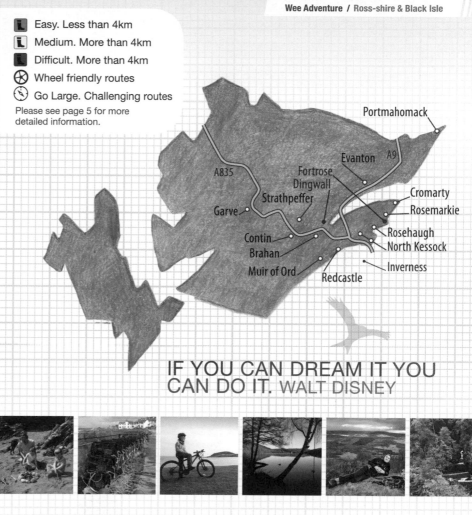

IF YOU CAN DREAM IT YOU CAN DO IT. WALT DISNEY

IRON AGE FORT, ORD HILL

Ord Hill sits proudly surveying Inverness from the edge of the Black Isle. It's a popular walking and mountain biking spot with a large free car park, clearly marked Forestry Commission Scotland walking routes and an information board.

fun fact

Ord Hill has a permanent orienteering course. For a free course map, visit www.britishorienteering.org.uk and search for Ord Hill.

PLAY IS THE **HIGHEST** FORM OF RESEARCH. ALBERT EINSTEIN

Ord Hill, near North Kessock

Trees and rocky outcrops make it easy to imagine our ancestors raiding and protecting this ancient hill. Ord means 'rounded hill' in Gaelic, and the remains of a 2000+ year old Iron Age Fort sit at the top of it.

Walk 1. Iron Age Fort trail

Steady inclines for the first half, then all downhill. 2.5km loop (red trail). The red trail takes you up to the site of an Iron Age fort where some stones still remain. For the first half, this adventure is all uphill but it's short and sharp, then all downhill again.

Walk 2. Ord Hill circular ⊗

Steady inclines, downhill and flat sections. 3.8km loop (blue trail). Off-road pram, wheelchair and standard bike. This trail is all along a wide forestry track circling the bottom of the hill. There are breaks in the trees for some great views of the Moray Firth. This route passes a Christmas tree plantation too.

directions 🚗

Inverness 5 miles. Take the A9 north. After the Kessock Bridge, take the exit signed to North Kessock. At the roundabout take the exit signed to Inverness A9 and Kilmuir. Go under the bridge and take the left turn signed to Drumsmital and Kilmuir. Take the next right to Kilmuir. You will then see Forestry Commission signs to Ord Hill, follow them up to the right. Postcode area IV1 3YF.

amenities ☕ 🛝

North Kessock (2 miles) has a hotel serving food, a shop, café and play park. It is well known for dolphin spotting on the banks of the Beauly Firth and a RNLI lifeboat station.

what it's great for

WALK TO AN IRON AGE FORT SITE

A FAMILY FRIENDLY CYCLE LOOP

WATCH SPECTACULAR SUNSETS

SEE WHERE CHRISTMAS TREES GROW

TAKE IN WONDERFUL VIEWS

ORD HILL
Furthest distance from Inverness 8km / 5miles

walk options
Walk 1. 2.5km 🄻
Walk 2. 3.8km 🄻

HIDDEN LOCH, NEAR NORTH KESSOCK

A narrow loch side path to navigate, rocky outcrops with big views and fields and woodland to dash about in. Family walks local to Inverness don't get much better than this.

Pitlundie

This adventure will challenge younger ones but it is so varied with some exciting distractions, the whole family are sure to enjoy it. Grownups will give it the thumbs up too, with amazing 360 degree views.

the walk

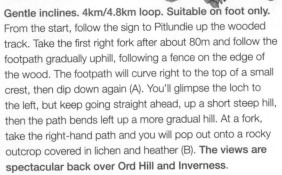

Gentle inclines. 4km/4.8km loop. Suitable on foot only.
From the start, follow the sign to Pitlundie up the wooded track. Take the first right fork after about 80m and follow the footpath gradually uphill, following a fence on the edge of the wood. The footpath will curve right to the top of a small crest, then dip down again (A). You'll glimpse the loch to the left, but keep going straight ahead, up a short steep hill, then the path bends left up a more gradual hill. At a fork, take the right-hand path and you will pop out onto a rocky outcrop covered in lichen and heather (B). **The views are spectacular back over Ord Hill and Inverness**.

Continue along the ridge on the small winding path through trees, for about 800m. There is a T-junction then a fork in the path, take the right path both times to stay up on the ridge. The path will narrow and eventually winds down to a

T junction with a grass vehicle track (C). Look right and walk to the gate for a great view of the Moray Firth over fields.

Now, walk back up the track away from the gate. From (C) you can **extend the route by 800m up to a fantastic 360 view point taking in the loch, the Black Isle, Ben Wyvis, Munlochy Bay and the Moray and Beauly Firth.** To extend the walk, take the first right off the vehicle track after about 80m, up a narrow grass path and follow it as it wiggles uphill. At the top of a short steep climb, turn left and you'll pop out at the top of a small summit (D).

Or, start to loop back from (C) by walking to the end of the vehicle track and turning left onto the tarmac road. Take the first left through two gates and walk down the left hand side of the grazing field. You'll see Loch Lundie open up in front of you. **Did you spot the treehouse?**

Go through a small wooden gate to walk back alongside the loch edge, starting on a wooden walk way (E). Follow this path straight on, through the little glen of trees and you will eventually find yourself back at point (A). Turn right at this junction and follow your footsteps back to the start.

enjoy the view

The path alongside the loch by the water is narrow and you may wish to hold the hands of younger children. Where the walk passes through the open field with livestock please put dogs on leads and shut gates properly.

© Crown copyright 2017 Ordnance Survey 100058484

what it's great for

SPOT RED KITES AND
OTHER BIRDS OF PREY

360 DEGREE VIEWS

WALK IN A MAGICAL LICHEN
COVERED FOREST

FIND A HIDDEN TREEHOUSE

cool fact

The plant that looks like a pale green beard covering many of the trees and rocks is called lichen. **Lichen** needs pure, unpolluted air to grow so abundantly and there is plenty of that here!

amenities

The nearby Munro's Nurseries, 2 miles, has a nice post-walk coffee shop for cake or lunch. It's on the B9161 to Munlochy. Postcode IV1 3XE.

directions 🚗

Inverness 6 miles. Take the A9 north. After the Kessock Bridge, take the exit signed to North Kessock and Kilmuir. At the roundabout take the exit signed to Inverness A9 and Kilmuir. Go under the bridge and take the left turn. Now follow signs to Kilmuir. You will pass Scottish Forestry Commission signs to Ord Hill on your right but keep going and take the next right to Kilmuir which has a dead end sign. On your left, 0.7 miles down this road, is a small layby and wooden walking sign to Pitlundie/Munlochy Bay. Park here. Postcode area IV1 3XG.

NATURE DOES NOT HURRY YET EVERYTHING IS ACCOMPLISHED.
LAO TZU

PITLUNDIE
Furthest distance from Inverness 10km / 6miles

walk options

Walk 1. 4km

Walk 2. 4.8km

BEACH DAY OUT, THE BLACK ISLE

Sweeping beaches and a woodland glen with waterfalls.

Rosemarkie, The Black Isle

The village is tucked away on the Black Isle on the Moray Firth. You can fill a whole day here with loads to explore, including a fairy glen with waterfalls, a sea cave and a peninsula with a lighthouse, famous for dolphin spotting. Rosemarkie beach is sandy with rock pools, a beach café, a play park and football pitch.

History tip. On the other side of the Moray Firth you can see Fort George, the mightiest artillery fortification in Britain. It was built after the Battle of Culloden to keep the Jacobites at bay. It is still an Army barracks and an exciting Historic Scotland site to visit.

'Who can be the first adventurer to spot the cave?'

Walk 1. Cairds Cave

Flat 3.5km return. Red trail on map. This is an out and back walk to a sea cave along the beach. From the start point, turn left along the path to the beach café, then drop down on to the beach (A). You can remain on the beach the whole way to the cave (B). Or, there is a grassy path to the back of the beach you can also use if the tide is high.

The cave entrance can get quite overgrown in the summer so it may not be obvious at first. It has a stream flowing near it and a distinctive stone cliff above it. Look out for peregrine falcons too.

Cave facts. The cave is thought to have been frequently inhabited by people and animals. A 2010 excavation of the site found animal bones dating to 600AD!

If the tide is out you can explore a second cave! On the beach, keep going around the corner through the jutting out rocks. Immediately on your left, look up into the side of the cliff.

walk 2. Dolphin Mile

Flat 5.5km loop (purple trail on map). 'Chanonry Point, the best place in Britain for dolphin-watching!' This walk loops around the peninsula. Chanonry Point lighthouse is the half way point, with information boards and picnic tables. **Dolphin spotting is best on a rising tide but you can get lucky any time.**

'Can you spot Fort George in the distance?'

From the start, drop down onto the beach, turn right and walk the Dolphin Mile to the lighthouse (A). Cross over the car park and join the path down the other side of the peninsula (B). At the end of the golf course (C) turn right and walk along this small road (Wester Green Gates). Turn left at the road end, then turn right onto Ness Road East. Follow this road through the golf club and back down to the beach.

tips

To save little legs, you can also drive and park directly at Chanonry Point. The point is pram and wheelchair friendly. Follow the shoreline road past the campsite and take the small road left through the golf course. It is also signed from Fortrose off the A832.

It's fun to experience Chanonry Point by bike.

ROSEMARKIE

Furthest distance from Inverness 24km / 15miles

NO ACT OF KINDNESS, NO MATTER HOW SMALL, IS EVER WASTED. AESOP

walk options
Walk 1. 3.5km
Walk 2. 5.5km

BEACH DAY OUT, THE BLACK ISLE

A great day out for the whole family to enjoy.

walk 3. The Fairy Glen

Slight inclines. 3km return (blue trail on map). When you step into the lush green of this glen cut out of sandstone rock, it is very easy to imagine the fairies that live among the bluebells and wash in the waterfalls when the humans are not looking. Maybe you can spot one? This walk is sheltered though it can get muddy underfoot.

From the start, walk through the village to the Fairy Glen car park where the route is signed from an RSPB information board (or park here). It is an out and back walk following the river all the way, past the pond, and ends at the second big waterfall. **Look out for the log full of real money at the top pool and make your wish to the fairies.**

walk 4. beach loop

Short beach walk. 1km loop (green trail on map). From the start, walk past the beach café and play park until you see steps going up the cliff side. Climb the steps and turn right at the top down a tree-lined path. It's a gentle meander downhill for about 300m until you reach a bench and here you rejoin onto the beach. Turn right and walk back along the beach to the café. Or, continue along the path and link into walk 1.

amenities

Right on the beach is the community run **Rosemarkie Beach Café and Exhibition** which sells homemade cake, light lunches and beach toys. It is open all year (weekends only Oct-Apr). There are lots of outdoor tables so you can bring your own picnic too.

Next to the café is a small sandy play park and a grass football pitch.

In the village, Crofters Bistro is a family-friendly restaurant. The Groam House Museum of Celtic and Pictish Art is free to enter (seasonal).

Woof! The beach café is very dog friendly (bowls of dog water, shade and a dog treat available!) but please keep dogs on leads on the grass and beach area outside the café.

On the way home. Fortrose Village. Fortrose is next door to Rosemarkie on the A832. The little harbour is a nice spot for eating an alfresco 'chippy,' from the popular fish and chip shop on the main street. There are other places to sit in and eat too. The partial ruin of the 12th century Fortrose Cathedral is also free to walk around.

'A rustle in the wind reminds us a fairy is near'
~ author unkown

pond life

Observe wildlife in an RSPB reserve.

rspb giving nature a home Scotland

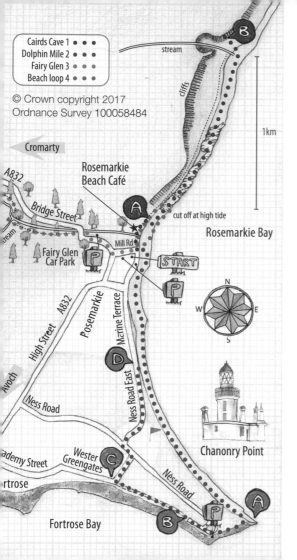

Cairds Cave 1 • • •
Dolphin Mile 2 • • •
Fairy Glen 3 • • •
Beach loop 4 • • •

© Crown copyright 2017
Ordnance Survey 100058484

Cromarty

A832

Rosemarkie
Beach Café

Bridge Street

Fairy Glen
Car Park

Mill Rd

cut off at high tide

Rosemarkie Bay

stream

cliffs

1km

START

Rosemarkie Beach Café — A

Posemarkie

High Street

A832

Ness Road

Avoch

Marine Terrace

Ness Road East

D

N
W   E
S

Chanonry Point

Wester
Greengates

C

cademy Street

rtrose

Ness Road

B

P

A

Fortrose Bay

directions

Inverness 15 miles. Take the A9 north. 2 miles after the Kessock bridge, turn right off the dual carriageway onto the B9161 signed to Munlochy. Turn right out of Munlochy to join the A832 which leads to Rosemarkie. Postcode area IV10 8UF.

Rosemarkie. You can park for free in the village or along the small road that fronts the beach called Marine Terrace. There is also a designated free car park at the start of the Fairy Glen. There is also parking at **Chanonry Point** (see walk 2).

what it's great for

BOULDER ON HUGE ROCKS

WALK ALONG THE BEACH

BE ENCHANTED BY WATERFALLS

TAKE A DIP IN THE BAY

DAM SMALL BEACH STREAMS

Great mountain biking at nearby Learnie Red Rocks. Learnie Red Rocks has miles of bike trails to suit all abilities. A map of the trails can be found on **www.scotland.forestry.gov.uk** It's Forestry Commission Scotland owned, so well signed with free parking. Continue on the A832 towards Cromarty for 3 miles and it's on the right.

ROSEMARKIE
Furthest distance from Inverness 24km / 15miles

walk options

Walk 3. 3km
Walk 4. 1km

51

CLIFFS, COVES & HISTORY

Discover coves, walk around cliffs and explore an ancient fishing village.

Cromarty

On the very tip of the Black Isle, Cromarty has exciting expeditions around cliffs, down to a hidden cove and gentler options around village lanes. There is a working harbour, lighthouse and a wide foreshore which is mostly pebbled but sandy in places with a grass common behind it. You'll also find a lively arts and food scene.

Cromarty history

Kids will be able to feel history all around them in Cromarty, without having to walk very far. A storm in 2012 exposed parts of the **12th century ancient royal burgh**. The ongoing archaeological dig site is sometimes exposed, alongside the South Sutors Walk (see map). Cromarty has a working Stevenson lighthouse from 1846. The village was once bustling around this natural port, with tales of international trade in hemp, a herring boom, a naval port and an oil boom.

Cromarty Firth was key to the defence of Britain during both world wars. A war ship, **HMS Natal**, blew up nearby in 1915 and remains of the wreckage still sit under the water. If you choose to do the South Sutor walk, you'll pass an intact **World War 1 gun emplacement**.

There are historical information boards dotted around the village. The Court House Museum is free to enter (open afternoons, Easter to mid-October).

'What's that over there?!' Over the bay, you can't fail to notice **Nigg Bay** and the oil drilling rigs brought here from the North Sea to be refurbished.

Why do artists and authors love Cromarty? Cromarty is a hub for many artists and cultural events. The crime writer Ian Rankin comes here to write many of his novels.

Take a sketch pad. Find a quiet spot and let the artist in you go for a few minutes. Or, make up your own story – what adventures may have happened to you if you'd lived here 200 years ago?

what it's great for

LET YOUR INNER ARTIST BE INSPIRED

WALK TO A SECRET ARCH BY THE SEA

CLIMB 100 STEPS UP TO THE SOUTH SUTOR

EXPLORE THE LANES OF A 700 YEAR OLD VILLAGE

GO BEACH COMBING

IF NOTHING EVER CHANGED THERE'D BE NO BUTTERFLIES.

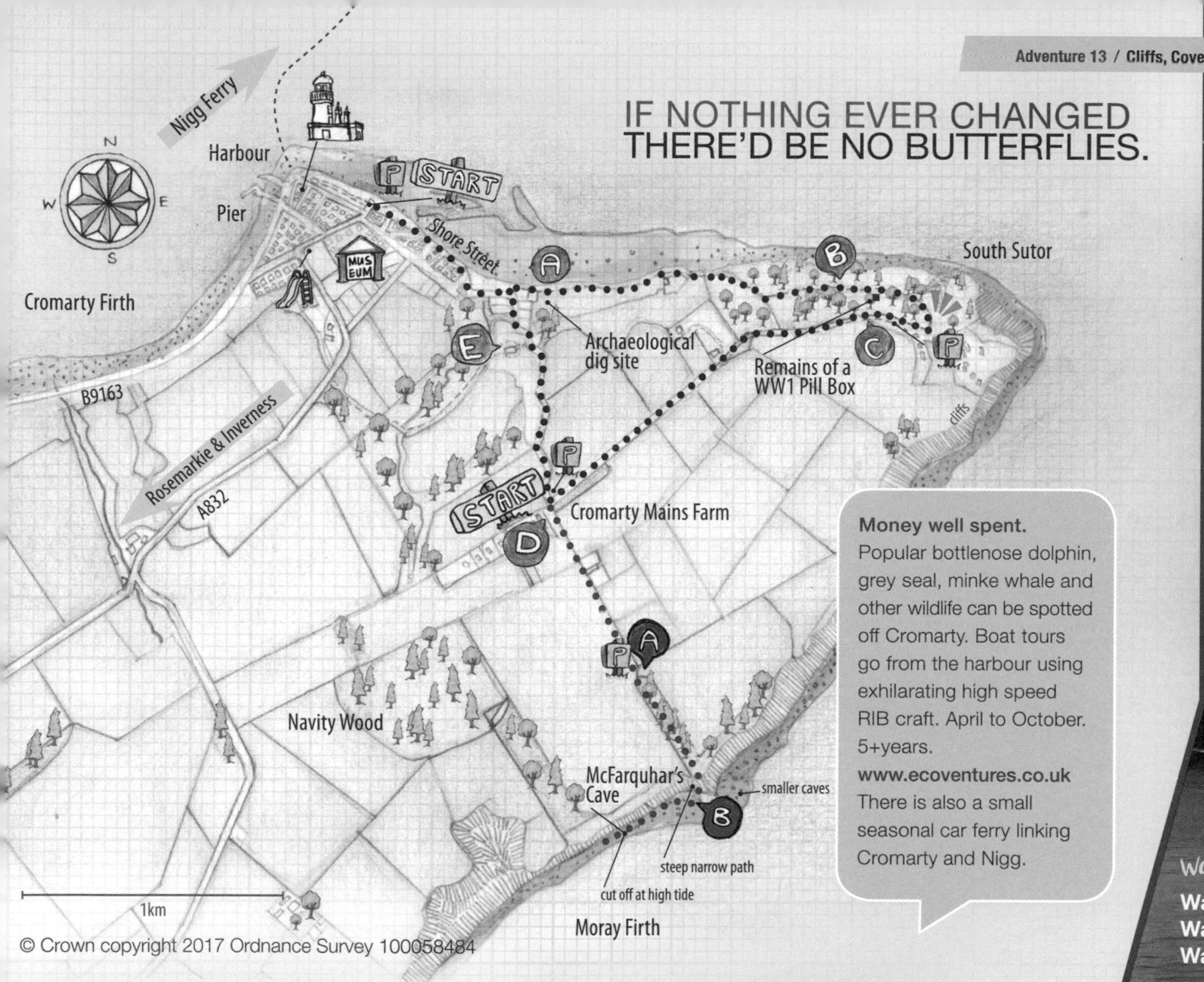

Nigg Ferry

Harbour

Pier

Cromarty Firth

B9163

Rosemarkie & Inverness

A832

START

Shore Street

MUSEUM

E

A

Archaeological dig site

B

South Sutor

C

Remains of a WW1 Pill Box

cliffs

START

Cromarty Mains Farm

D

Navity Wood

P A

McFarquhar's Cave

smaller caves

B

steep narrow path

cut off at high tide

Moray Firth

1km

© Crown copyright 2017 Ordnance Survey 100058484

CROMARTY

Furthest distance from Inverness 38km / 24miles

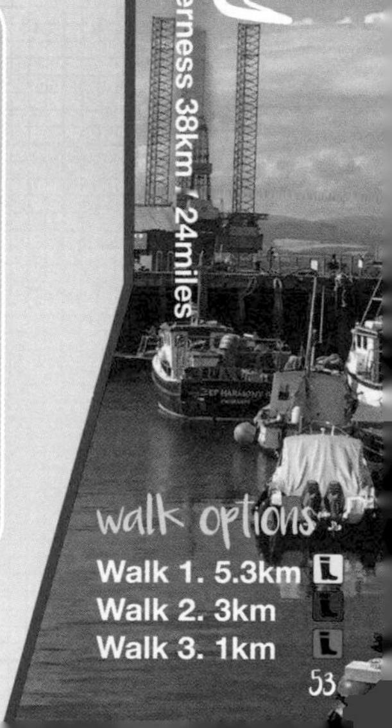

Money well spent.
Popular bottlenose dolphin, grey seal, minke whale and other wildlife can be spotted off Cromarty. Boat tours go from the harbour using exhilarating high speed RIB craft. April to October. 5+years.
www.ecoventures.co.uk
There is also a small seasonal car ferry linking Cromarty and Nigg.

walk options
Walk 1. 5.3km
Walk 2. 3km
Walk 3. 1km

53

CLIFFS, COVES & HISTORY

There are historical information boards dotted around the town.

walk 1. South Sutor

Gentle inclines, one long steep incline. 5.3km loop (blue route on map). Walk the South Sutor headland to the mouth of the Cromarty Firth. Do you count 100 steps as you walk up, up, up to a great view point? Then, loop back down to Cromarty.

Local folklore. Sutor is the Scots word for shoemaker. One story tells of two giant shoemakers, the Sutors, who used the north and south cliffs at the mouth of the Firth as their workbenches, and shared their tools back and forth between one another.

Walk along Shore Street with the Cromarty Firth on your left. The road curves right but take the small path signed left to South Sutor (A), by an information board. Continue along this narrow path, up into woods full of bluebells in spring and glorious colours in autumn. Keep the Firth on your left but about half way up the woods be careful not to miss the path forking right up to more steps (B) and a small **World War 1 gun emplacement**. Continue

around the headland, ending in a gravel car park area and viewpoint (C). Then, follow the wooden signs back down a quiet minor road to Cromarty Mains (D), then back into Cromarty village. You will pass **The Stables**, an artist studio and venue (E), sometimes open to the public. Listen out for the resident peacocks and say hello to the unicorn.

walk 2. MacFarquhar's Bed

One long steep incline. 3km return from Cromarty Mains (red route on map). This walk is varied and dramatic, taking you down to a stone beach with a giant arch coming out of the sea. The descent down the cliff side is narrow, winding and steep in parts so keep younger children close to an adult at this point. To save any walking on road, start the walk at Cromarty Mains where there are a few spaces for cars by the track side (see map). Postcode area IV11 8XS.

Walk up the farm track from **Cromarty Mains**, over the brow of the hill. The track leads into a wood full of huge dead trees (A). It's now downhill all the way to sea level. The path takes a slight right (ignore the sign to the left), taking you down the cliff side between gorse bushes to the beach (B). At the bottom it's fun to explore the bothy, fossil hunt and rock scramble. The bothy has an outside fire pit for use. Return the way you came, allowing time for it to take longer than on the way down!

extension to walks 1. and 2.

The **South Sutor loop** passes the start point to **MacFarquhar's Bed**, so you can combine both walks (8.5km loop from village, see map on page 53).

walk 3. exploring the village ⊗

Flat, small inclines. 1km loop. The village lanes are pram and wheelchair friendly however the paths up to the Hugh Millar statue are cobbles, dirt and gravel. The village isn't big and it's nice to meander through the lanes (vennels). The harbour, the lighthouse and the old ice house

are good to see along the front. To the back of the village, at the top of a medieval lane called The Paye, look for the tall statue of a famous local **fossil hunter** called **Hugh Millar** and an interesting graveyard. A gentle short woodland walk, signed Ladies Walk, leads from opposite the statue.

amenities

Cromarty has pubs and numerous good cafés. **Couper's Creek** on Church Street is great for ice cream and cake. Sutor's Creek is a scrummy pizzeria by the harbour. There is also a pottery, book shop, cheese shop and some interesting gift and antique shops. It has a good, central play park and public toilets.

directions to Cromarty 🚗

Inverness 24 miles. Take the A9 north. After the Kessock Bridge, turn right after 2 miles onto the B9161 signed to Munlochy. Turn right out of Munlochy to join the A832 which leads to Rosemarkie then on through to Cromarty. Postcode area IV11 8XA. Park in the free designated area off Shore Street on the seafront.

CROMARTY

Furthest distance from Inverness 38km / 24miles

walk options

Walk 1. 5.3km
Walk 2. 3km
Walk 3. 1km

COUNTRY ESTATES, ROSS-SHIRE

Nestled away in the Highlands are many grand old country estates. Most are working farms with beautiful buildings, landscaping and great footpaths to explore. Here are three with freedom to roam and enjoy some genteel countryside.

what it's great for

DISCOVER A MEDIEVAL CASTLE SITE

PICNIC BY A PICTURESQUE POND

STAND ON THE RUINS OF AN 18TH CENTURY ESTATE HOUSE

WALK ALONG THE BANKS OF THE RIVER CONON

EXPLORE BEAUTIFUL COUNTRY SIDE

adventure tip

Please take care to remember the Scottish Outdoor Access Code; stick to paths, respect signs and keep dogs under control.

Most of these estates have obvious tracks and some of them have maps and/or waymarked routes too. Here are directions for parking, a short route option and things to look for. The main exploring is left to you!

Redcastle Estate, near North Kessock

Redcastle Estate has a real castle to gaze up at. Though it is crumbling and fenced off, it still has great charm. The first castle on this site was in medieval times and it was once the oldest inhabited castle in Scotland. It fell into disrepair after World War 2.

walk 1. castle route

Flat, firm track. 1km return (with more tracks to explore)
Some off-road pram and wheelchair friendly tracks.
Walk up the road through the small village. As the houses end, turn right onto a high tree lined track, past old stone gate posts and a gatekeeper's cottage. Eventually you'll cross a stone bridge. Here, fork left up a track past the stables for a 1km return woodland river side stroll. Or, fork right to the castle.

extensions to this walk

The track leading off beyond the castle goes straight for 1km, then drops down to the shore road, where you can loop back to the village.

cycle route option ⊗

Cycle from North Kessock village along the pretty shoreline road to Redcastle Estate, 7.5km one way. This flat, minor road has hedgerows full of wild flowers in the summer and great views over the Beauly Firth. The routes also link to Inverness city cycle paths without going on main roads (see useful links on page 107).

amenities

North Kessock has a shop, tea room and hotel. The harbour is a sea life watching hub.

directions

Inverness 10 miles. Take the A9 north. Take the first exit after the Kessock bridge to North Kessock, then turn left at the roundabout down into North Kessock village. Turn right at the village hall onto Marine Park. Follow this road all the way along the shore for 4.5 miles to Redcastle village. Park on the left by the red phone box, in a designated free parking and picnic area. Postcode IV6 7SG.

A SMILE IS HAPPINESS YOU'LL FIND RIGHT UNDER YOUR NOSE. TOM WILSON

ESTATES
Furthest distance from Inverness 26km / 16miles

walk option
Walk 1. 1km

COUNTRY ESTATES, ROSS-SHIRE

There used to be over 2000 castles in Scotland; around 600 are still standing.

Rosehaugh, Blackisle

Rosehaugh Estate has tracks galore, a pond with swans, the ruins of an 18th century estate house and gardens, and is known for a glorious snowdrop display in February.

walk 2. route to the ruins

Tarmac, one long incline. 2km return (with more tracks to explore). This estate has bike, off-road pram and wheelchair friendly routes. The road up to the ruin is fully tarmac. There is a useful map board of the estate's public rights of way in the parking area. Follow the quiet single track

road into the estate grounds, alongside a stream, then uphill through trees (look for fairy doors in some of them on your right). Eventually you'll reach a massive stone veranda. It has views of Black Isle farmland and the remains of a landscaped garden. The very grand Rosehaugh House was knocked

down in 1959. From the ruin, you can continue to explore tracks to the right and behind the ruin into woodland.

cycle route option ⊗

Cycle all the way into Avoch along these estate tracks (see map board in car park). From Avoch it is also possible to cycle along the old railway line into Fortrose. Visit **www.transitionblackisle.org** to plan your route.

amenities

Munlochy has a family friendly pub serving food, the Allangrange Arms. Avoch has a shop, takeaway and hotel serving food called The Old Railway.

directions 🚗

Inverness 11 miles. Take the A9 north. Turn right to Munlochy on the B9161. Once through Munlochy, turn right at the T junction onto the A832. After 2 miles, look for a sign to the left, for Rosehaugh Estate. Take this and park in the free parking area immediately on the right.

I WISH YOU JOY WITH ALL MY HEART. JANE AUSTEN

'I don't think limits.' Usain Bolt

Brahan Estate, near Dingwall

Brahan Estate has a walk down to the River Conon, past a giant walled garden, streams, a beautiful pond and through ancient woodland.

walk 3. The Dell river walk

Flat, firm vehicle tracks. 2km return (with more tracks to explore). Off-road pram and wheelchair friendly. **Standard bike.** The Dell route to the river is signed from the car park. It is mostly a wide vehicle track. Or, small wooden arrows to the left give the option to take mini detours from this track; along winding paths by a burn, under giant trees, over foot bridges, logs to scramble and a pet graveyard to discover. The pond becomes obvious on your right, slightly off the main track. **Have a picnic on giant rocks or walk right around it.** Back on the main track, keep going as it curves left to reach the wide River Conon. It's possible to walk in either direction along the river bank (turn left for approx 2.5km to Dunglass Island, an accessible island in the middle of the river).

Infamous. Brahan is world famous for **Brahan Seer**, an estate labourer from the 1600's who made accurate predictions on the future. He foresaw in detail the fall of the seat of Seaforth (Clan Mackenzie) and was executed when it came true.

See more. This estate welcomes visitors. Download a map and get more information. **brahan.com/walking**

Visit. Tollie Red Kites is a partnership between RSPB Scotland and the Brahan Estate (see page 62).

Fact. The view from the pond up a tree lined avenue is of the estate house, which was once the stables to **Brahan Castle**. The castle is no longer there but was the seat of the **Clan MacKenzie** in Jacobite times.

amenities

Dingwall town has free parking and all amenities. Or, see Pictish Discoveries (see page 60).

Something different. Dingwall Auction Mart, on the left just before entering Dingwall town has the Drovers café, antique sales and a viewing area to watch the animal sales.

directions

Inverness 16 miles. Take the A9 north. At Tore roundabout, take the A835 to Ullapool. Stay on this road. Brahan Estate is signed on the left with a big white sign, two miles past the next roundabout. Postcode area IV7 8EE. To park, go left at the first T junction, past the estate offices. Take the right fork at the end of this lane and go right again. There are signs for a camping area. Follow this road for about 200m to a cross roads. Turn right to the Dell Walk and park here on the left.

ESTATES
Furthest distance from Inverness 26km / 16miles

walk options
Walk 2. 2km
Walk 3. 2km

PICTISH DISCOVERIES

Strathpeffer is surprising! Discover a maze, hillfort, lochs, mountain bike trails and loads of history.

Strathpeffer

Walk to a stone maze, then up the Cat's Back to a Pictish hillfort to take in massive views. Test your mountain bike skills in the woodland and hills behind Strathpeffer and Contin. Circumnavigate a loch. Explore a Victorian spa village to discover the Pictish Eagle Stone and giant carvings of legends.

walk 1. maze and hill ⊗

Touchstone Maze, the Cat's Back and Knock Farril hillfort (also known as Knockfarrel). Medium 3-7km return. Walk 1 is split into three legs. Leg 1 – off-road pram and wheelchair and standard bike friendly. Legs 2 and 3 – mountain bike friendly. You can return the way you came after any suggested leg. On a clear day, there are great views of **Ben Wyvis**, the mountains in the west, the **Cromarty Firth** and **Loch Ussie**. This area is well known for spotting red kites (bird of prey).

Leg 1. Blackmuir Woods car park to Touchstone Maze. Hard packed stone paths, some muddy areas, with small inclines. 3km return. Follow the Forestry Commission Scotland green trail from the Blackmuir Woods car park for 1.5km, following signs to

the Touchstone Maze. The maze is made of 81 rocks of different ages and types, taken from all over the Highlands and Islands, designed in the style of a prehistoric labyrinth.

Fun to climb on and hide around!

Leg 2. Touchstone Maze, up the Cat's Back.
Hard packed dirt and grass paths, undulating with one steep uphill section. Additional 2km return. Continue on the green trail behind the maze for 150m. Turn left at the first junction, and right at the fork for 30m, then straight over the cross road in the track following a large wooden signpost to Knockfarrel (you've now left the green trail). This steep short path leads to a gap in some stones on a dip (saddle) between two high points on the Cat's Back. **Look down on Loch Ussie**. Turn immediately left through the wishing gate and walk up and along the ridge for about 400m, until you reach a black stone marker with a symbol of three people hugging.

enjoy the view

60

walk 1. maze and hill continued

Leg 3. Cat's Back to Knock Farril (Pictish Iron Age hillfort site). Grass and dirt paths along an undulating ridge. Additional 2km return. From the black stone marker, keep following the path along the ridge. It dips down to a parking area with a picnic table and historical information board, then up to Knock Farril hillfort site. **Picts reigned here from as early as 800BC; remains of the walls are still clear but the final fort was probably destroyed by a big fire.**

Return options. Return the way you came or take a lower level path. From the Knock Farril parking area, facing back to Strathpeffer, take the path going gently downhill along the right side of the ridge. It will level out and re-join the green post trail back to the Touchstone Maze.

Tip to save little legs. To reach the Knock Farril parking area by car, follow the directions below to Strathpeffer but take the right turn signed **Tollie Red Kites**, Knockfarrel and Lochussie off the A385, four miles before Contin.

amenities

Strathpeffer village centre has a small shop, deli bakery, cafés and hotels (some seasonal). Visit **Square Wheels** for bike hire and maintenance in the village square. Also, public toilets, free parking and information boards.

what its great for

CLIMB TO A PICTISH IRON AGE HILLFORT

DISCOVER THE MYTH OF THE EAGLE STONE

CYCLE OR WALK AROUND A PRETTY LOCH

PLAY IN A CONCENTRIC MAZE

EXPLORE A VICTORIAN SPA VILLAGE

STRATHPEFFER
Furthest distance from Inverness 29km / 18miles

walk options

Walk 1.	3-7km
1.	3km
1+2.	5km
1+2+3.	7km

LET US STEP INTO THE NIGHT AND PURSUE THAT FLIGHTY TEMPTRESS, ADVENTURE. J.K ROWLING

PICTISH DISCOVERIES

The mountain looking down over Strathpeffer is Ben Wyvis.
It is the 85th highest Munro at 1046 metres.

history fact

Choo choo! There was once a bustling steam train line to Strathpeffer, it brought health seekers to the spa (find out more in the Pump Room museum, village centre, free, seasonal opening). In WW1 and WW2, troops and war casualties were brought by train to the village. Now, The Old Station, 200m from the village centre, has a café, gift shop, picnic area, an easy walk/cycle along the old railway line (The Peffery Way to Dingwall), free parking and the Highland Museum of Childhood (seasonal opening, small entry fee).

rspb giving nature a home Scotland

Visit Tollie Red Kites RSPB area near Strathpeffer. Enjoy close-up views of these beautiful birds feeding. There is a disabled access viewing area in a bothy, an exhibition and a creative space for kids to draw. Open daily. Feeding times 1.30pm winter, 2.30pm summer. www.rspb.org.uk

Stathpeffer Spa Village

When sulphurous springs were discovered in the 1700's, what was farmland grew into a famous Victorian health spa destination until the 1920's.

walk 2. the village ⊗

Good packed gravel and tarmac footpaths. 1km loop. Standard pram and wheelchair. However, the final 10m section to Eagle Stone is on a very narrow, dirt path. Start in the village square and **explore the gardens behind Strathpeffer Spa Pavilion; wooded paths, a stream and carved wooden giants**. Then, cross the road in front of the pavilion and turn right. Go past Strathpeffer Hotel, then turn left up the side road signed to the **Eagle Stone**. It's a 300m walk to the stone, a 7th century relic from the Picts.

> Find out why you wouldn't want to push the stone over, unless you really like swimming!

Now, return the way you came. Turn left on the main road to explore The Old Station (see Choo Choo!). Loop back to the pavilion along the main street.

walk 3. Loch Kinellan ⊗

Undulating hard packed stone and dirt forest track, one short steep hill. 2.7km loop. Off-road pram and wheelchair and standard bike friendly. This lovely signed circuit goes past farmland and forest with hill views. The loch is home to lots of water birds. If you want a longer outing, this loop links into other signed paths for Contin Woods (2.8km), a viewpoint (0.5km), and popular mountain bike trails for exploring.

directions

To Strathpeffer. Inverness 18 miles. Take the A9 north. At the Tore roundabout, take the 2nd exit onto the A835, following signs to Ullapool. Stay on the A835 until Contin village. Just inside Contin, take the right turn signed to Strathpeffer on the A834. The village square has free parking. Postcode area IV14 9DW.

Walk 1 start (Blackmuir Woods). Just as you enter Strathpeffer from Contin, the Forestry Commission Scotland car park for Blackmuir Woods is a a right turn by the sign for West Park. A small green walking sign to Knockfarrel points the way. Postcode area IV14 9BT.

Walk 3 start (Loch Kinellan). Just as you enter Strathpeffer from Contin, Loch Kinellan is signed on the left, on a 'no through road' sign. Follow this road up and almost at the end, a green pathway sign points left to the Loch Kinellan circuit and free car park. Postcode area IV14 9ET.

STRATHPEFFER
Furthest distance from Inverness 29km / 18miles

walk options

Walk 2. 1km
Walk 3. 2.7km

SPECTACULAR WATERFALLS

Spot salmon leaping! It has been said this is one of the best places in Scotland to see salmon migrating upriver.

But why do salmon need ladders?! Cross the swing bridge, tun left and walk up alongside a salmon ladder to see how salmon still make their amazing journey upstream when the waterfall is too strong to leap.

Rogie Falls, Contin

Wet Weather

This is a short walk that packs in plenty of drama! Paths through ancient birch and alpine woodland lead to a suspension bridge over a deep gully with close up views of a crashing waterfall and a salmon ladder. The two Forestry Commission Scotland trails are mostly under trees and alongside and over the Black Water river.

walk 1. Riverside trail [green]

Slight inclines 1.3km loop. Only suitable on foot. The green trail is the most interesting with some great boulders for scrambling and a mossy glen, before dropping alongside the river and looping round to the swing bridge.

walk 2. Salmon trail [red]

Some inclines. 800m return. Off-road pram and wheelchair friendly. This is a direct route to the waterfall viewing area.

Go further! Cross the bridge (some steps) and you can explore Torrachilty Forest tracks for miles. Turn left, and take the clear path that veers gently up at an angle into the woods.

what it's great for

GOOD VIEWS OF BEN WYVIS

BRIDGE OVER DRAMATIC WATERFALLS

PICTURESQUE FOREST WALKS TO EXPLORE

SALMON LEAPING FROM JULY TO SEPTEMBER

HUNTING FOR FAIRIES IN CONTIN

amenities

Public toilet (seasonal opening) in the car park. Contin has a village store.

directions

Inverness 19 miles. Take the A9 north. At the Tore roundabout take the A835 road to Ullapool. Drive through Contin village on the A835 and Rogie Falls signed car park is on your right about 2 miles on from the village. There is free parking. Postcode IV14 9EQ (Contin area).

This road leads to the start of the walk up Ben Wyvis. See the **Go Large adventure** (page 91) if you're tempted to try a little bit of it or want to go for bagging a Munro!

Fairy Hunt at Coul House

Don't just drive through Contin because there are fairies to be found! The gorgeous Coul House Hotel has a fairy trail through ancient giant pines and rhododendrons. Can you find the fairy butterfly dell, the Christmas fairy, the giant spiders and many, many more? This will amuse all ages and that's a promise. The hotel is perfect for a treat post-walk hot chocolate or cream tea. You are still welcome to use the fairy trail without using the hotel facilities.

Directions. Coul House Hotel is signed to the left, in the centre of Contin, heading back towards Inverness, 0.5 miles up a small road.

Loch Achility, Contin

This is a **beautiful spot for a picnic** and to potter or paddle on stone shores of a great loch.

Directions. Drive out of Contin on the A835 towards Rogie Falls. Just past the village, turn left onto a minor road, signed to Loch Achility. Continue on this road for about 2 mile, until signs for a Forestry Commission Scotland car park and picnic area on the left.

facts

Scottish salmon are amazing. By the time they reach Rogie Falls they have swum all the way upstream, heading home to the exact place where they were born, to lay their own eggs. They 'smell,' their home, even after four years away feeding in the Atlantic Ocean or North Sea! Where were you born? How long do you think it would take to walk there and would you know the way?

MY HEART'S IN THE HIGHLANDS WHEREVER I GO. ROBERT BURNS

ROGIE FALLS

Furthest distance from Inverness 30km / 19miles

walk options

Walk 1. 1.3km
Walk 2. 800m

65

DEEP RAVINES, HEATHERY HILLTOPS

Stay low and play in a fantastic community woodland play area and discover a deep river gorge. Or, climb up high through forest to a heathery hillside and a curious old monument.

Evanton & Fyrish, Ross-shire

A short detour off the A9 north, Evanton Wood has fantastic footpaths suitable for walks, biking and prams, with an area of community woodland including an adventure play area for families. Upstream, discover Black Rock Gorge, a deep, thin, Ice Age ravine. Close by, an adventure up to Fyrish Monument, a prominent feature on the hillside above the Cromarty Firth is well worth the effort.

Evanton Wood

Evanton Wood is an attractive area of mixed woodland alongside a river. In the area closest to the village is a free community woodland adventure playground, inviting everyone to build a camp, swing, balance, climb, tunnel, paddle and picnic.

Only 1km upstream from the adventure area is the mile long, deep ravine called the **Black Rock Gorge**, only 3.6m wide but up to 30m deep! Two foot bridges allow you to peer down into the gorge, where the stream can

be heard but hardly seen. The gorge appears in 'Harry Potter and the Goblet of Fire'! There are also secret trails, an esker ridge path and pond area to discover.

walk 1. adventure area ⊗

Slightly undulating on hard packed paths. 1.2km return. Standard bike, pram and wheelchair friendly. Disabled car users can park right beside the adventure play area, using the same access point (gravel road). From the start point, walk 100m up Chapel Road (by the Co-op) and turn first right to the end of Camden Street. Follow the dark green path signs to Evanton Wood (500m and Black Rock Gorge 1.6km). This track goes past some houses, through a metal gate and 100m on to the adventure play area. You can also walk down to the river behind the cabin by a choice of paths.

enjoy the view

Have your own campfire! Evanton Community Wood invites families to use the ready-made fire pits for a campfire. Scavenge for your own firewood. Have a responsible adult on fire safety watch and take all your rubbish home please.

WHERE'S THE FUN
WITHOUT A BIT OF RISK?
J.K. ROWLING

walk 2. Black Rock Gorge ⊗

Undulating on clear paths, some muddy areas. 3.4km return. Suitable for mountain bikes. There is a map board (and usually free printed maps to borrow) by the adventure area in Evanton Wood. Start by following walk 1 directions to the adventure area, then facing the map board, take the downhill righthand fork, signed to **Black Rock Gorge**. It's a clear path, keeping the river on the right, with one signed right turn down a steep path to the first footbridge. At the first of two footbridges, cross and turn left. Cross the second footbridge and turn left again, back towards the first footbridge and join the original path back to the adventure area.

Alternative return. The map board suggests a slightly longer return loop taking in the pond area and an esker ridge path. As you retrace your steps downhill on the main path, take the first turn right to the pond decking area, then left and left again.

> **Get thinking.** Can you name 20 things we use in everyday life made from trees?

what its great for

WALK UP TO A CURIOUS, HUGE MONUMENT

PEER INTO THE MISTY DEPTHS OF A RAVINE

BUILD YOUR OWN DEN

WHEEL FRIENDLY WOODLAND PATHS

EXPLORE A UNIQUE PLAY AREA

EVANTON & FYRISH
Furthest distance from Inverness 22km / 35miles

walk options
Walk 1. 1.2km
Walk 2. 3.4km

DEEP RAVINES, HEATHERY HILLTOPS

Fyrish Monument's giant stone arches keep watch over the entire length of the Cromarty Firth out to the North Sea.

history

The monument was built in 1783 by a local laird who had been a commander of British Forces in India but returned to the Highlands during the Clearances (see page 35, Explore a Glen). Many local people were starving and he provided paid work to build this monument.

Fyrish Monument, near Alness

A steady uphill walk, through sheltered evergreen forest full of heather, moss and lichen, with a stream and footbridge to cross. The hillside feels excitingly remote – lie down in the heather to sky gaze. On a windy day the arches are great to sit under for a sheltered picnic.

walk 3. Fyrish Monument ⊗

Steep inclines on hard packed forest track, some uneven sections. 6km return. Suitable for mountain bikes. **The Jubilee Trail** is signed from the car park; simply follow it straight on uphill through forest for the first 2km, taking no turns or forks. The forest thins out as you pass a small lochan (listen out for frogs), onto open heathery hillside. From there it's about 500m on a gentle incline to the monument. Who can see it first? Return the way you came, downhill at twice the speed!

A WINNER IS A DREAMER WHO NEVER GIVES UP.
NELSON MANDELA

amenities

Evanton village has a shop and café. **The Storehouse** at Foulis is signed just off the A9 before Evanton. It's great for food and coffee, an outdoor play and seating area and seal spotting by the Cromarty Firth. Nearby **Dingwall** is an old market town with many amenities and easy free parking.

directions

Evanton Woods. Inverness 17 miles. Take the A9 north towards Tain. Cross the long Cromarty Bridge. About 2 miles after the bridge, turn left at the first sign to Evanton onto the B817 and keep following signs into the village. Park in the free car park in Evanton village centre on Balconie Street, opposite the shops. Postcode area IV16 9UN. www.evantonwood.com

Fyrish Monument, near Alness. Inverness 22 miles. This start point is 5 miles further on from Evanton. From the village centre, continue on the B817. Out of the village, turn left onto the B9176, Struie Road. After 1.5 miles, take the minor road signed Boath. The parking area is on the left after 1 mile, signed Novar Estate, Jubilee Trail. Postcode area IV17 0XL. Free parking, can get muddy!

EVANTON & FYRISH
Furthest distance from Inverness 22km / 35miles

walk options
Walk 3. 6km

EXPLORE A PENINSULA, PORTMAHOMACK

"

'This adventure all takes place on the Tarbat Ness Peninsula. Portmahomack is a fishing village with a great beach. A short drive away, the lighthouse is good for adventuring along dramatic coastal scenery.'

what it's great for

FISHING VILLAGE WITH A SANDY BEACH

RED AND WHITE LIGHTHOUSE

CLAMBER ON UNUSUAL ROCK FORMATIONS

SPOT SEA OTTERS

EXPLORE WILD COVES

facts

'Did the Vikings build sandcastles here too?' 'No, because they were too busy raiding!' Portmahomack is the site of the only Pictish monastery ever discovered, said to have been destroyed in a Viking raid in the year 800AD. The peninsula has witnessed many clashes between clans and king. Check out the Tarbat Discovery Centre (small charge). www.tarbat-discovery.co.uk

Portmahomack Village

Portmahomack sits at the start of the peninsula. It's a pretty fishing village with a stone wall harbour and a lovely sandy beach perfect for digging and pottering. The water is a clear sky blue on a calm day and it's a sheltered place to splash about in shallow waves if you can brave the nip of the North Sea waters.

walk 1. harbour and coastal path

Flat. 1-5km one way. Grassy paths and rocky shoreline, suitable on foot only. Explore some of the coastal path that leads 5km to Tarbat Ness lighthouse. From the centre of the village, the start of the footpath is just beyond the harbour and a car park, signed to 'Tarbat Ness 5km', through a gate.

See the **Go Large adventure** for more details of the entire 14km peninsula loop.

Good to know. Portmahomack beach is easy to access and you can park your car right next to it.

Keep going to ancient Dornoch town. The huge, sweeping sandy beach of Dornoch is 11 miles further north along the A9. Standing by Portmahomack harbour, you can see the golden sands over the water to your left. The beach has giant rocks to climb and miles of walking opportunities. Dornoch, an ancient Royal Burgh town, has plenty of amenities and even its own cathedral and castle.

amenities

There is a local shop on the beach front that has the usual essentials including ice cream, buckets and spades. The friendly, central Carnegie Café, just behind the beach front, sells hot food, drinks and ice cream cones.

directions

Portmahomack. Inverness 41 miles. Take the A9 north to Thurso/Tain for 29 miles. Take a signed right turn onto the B9165. Follow this for 10 miles following signs to Portmahomack. Free parking on the beach front. Postcode area IV20 1YE.

Tarbat Ness Lighthouse. Just beyond the Portmahomack village welcome sign, take the right turn signed to Tarbat Ness. The lighthouse is 3 miles straight on, at the end of the peninsula. Free car park 300m from the lighthouse. Postcode area IV20 1RD.

PORTMAHOMACK
Furthest distance from Inverness 65km / 41miles

walk options
Walk 1. 1-5km

"EXPLORE A PENINSULA, PORTMAHOMACK

The picture-perfect red and white Tarbat Ness Lighthouse stands on the tip of the peninsula and could come straight out of a Secret Seven story.

Tarbat Ness Lighthouse

Explore through the heather and rugged coastline that dips in and out of small sand and rock bays. It's easy to imagine smugglers and ship wrecks in days gone by.

It is wild and beautiful and you can spend a couple of hours clambering on the rocks, beach combing and enticing the kids to find out what is around the next cove... and the next.

Tarbat Ness is one of the best places locally to spot sea otters. Look carefully, one may be casually watching you as he floats about on his back. Dolphins and seals also stop by.

walk 2. lighthouse & coves

Flat. 1-3km return. Suitable on foot only. From the car park, go through the gate and head 300m down the straight lane towards the lighthouse. Explore the tip of the peninsula in an easy loop (A). There are lots of interesting rock formations to divert to and scramble over.

Once you've done that, walk back to the car park then along the stone wall lined road back in the direction of Portmahomack. Take the first left turn down to the water and an old stone slipway (B).

Go through the gate on the right into the field just before the slipway starts. Walk from here along the path that hugs the coastline or on the beach as far as you feel like. There is an obvious turn-around point where the beach has eroded away (C). Then retrace your steps.

I am rumoured to be built on a roman fortification site.

FROM THERE TO HERE, AND HERE TO THERE, FUNNY THINGS ARE EVERYWHERE. DR SEUSS

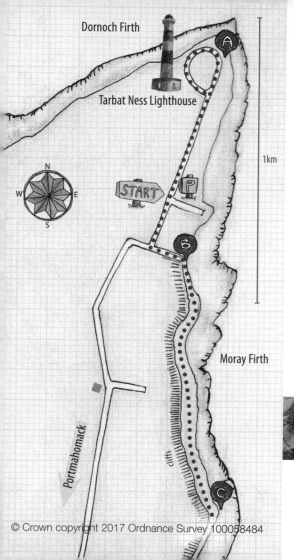

Dornoch Firth

Tarbat Ness Lighthouse

START

1km

N
W   E
S

Moray Firth

Portmahomack

cliffs

© Crown copyright 2017 Ordnance Survey 100058484

adventure tip!

Several sandy coves to the right of the stone slipway (B) are fun for making a small campfire. You need to bring your own firewood etc but there are usually some ready-made fire pits on the beach. Please take all your rubbish home.

cool fact

The lighthouse is 41m high with 203 steps to the top. It's one of the tallest in Britain. It was built in 1830 after one storm wrecked 16 boats off the peninsula. You can't go inside it but if you're here at dusk you will see it working.

calling young ornithologists!

The peninsula is a place of special interest for observing migratory birds. Many travel as far as Brazil to avoid a Scottish winter!

The tarmac lane from the car park to the lighthouse boundary (A) is suitable for wheelchairs and prams.

PORTMAHOMACK
Furthest distance from Inverness 65km / 41miles

walk options
Walk 2. 1-3km

NAIRNSHIRE & MORAY

58 **Wilderness Beach** > Whiteness, Nairn
L min 600m max 9km

60 **Perfect Beaches** > Nairn, Findhorn,
Culbin, Roseisle, Cummingston
⊗ L L L min 1km max 19km

L Easy. Less than 4km
L Medium. More than 4km
L Difficult. More than 4km
⊗ Wheel friendly routes
🕒 Go Large. Challenging routes
Please see page 5 for more
detailed information.

Findhorn   Roseisle   Cummingston
Nairn   Culbin   Lossiemouth
Whiteness

A96

Nairnshire
& Moray

Inverness

MAY YOU ALWAYS HAVE A SHELL IN YOUR
POCKET AND SAND BETWEEN YOUR TOES.

WILDERNESS BEACH, WHITENESS

A huge expanse of fine white sand on the Moray Firth. Beautifully deserted, it will be you and a couple of other dog walkers at most.

Whiteness Beach, near Nairn

This discovery begins with a 300m walk down a grass track between gorse bushes towards the shore. The beach opens in front of you with views to the Black Isle across the water.

walk 1. fisherman's hut

Flat 7km return along the shore. Once on the beach turn left to walk to the fisherman's hut, towards Whiteness Point. Or, stay where you are and the beach is your oyster!

walk 2. Nairn harbour

Flat 9km return. Turn right along the beach and walk all the way to Nairn along the coast past the golf course when the tide is low. Free parking at both ends.

RUNNING WILD,
BAREFOOT
AND FREE!

directions

Inverness 13 miles. Take the road to Nairn/Aberdeen from Inverness (A96).

About 2 miles before Nairn, you will see a sign left to Whiteness but ignore that turn! Take the next left turn signed to Ardersier on the B9092.

Take the first right down a single track road, not signed. This leads to some farm buildings. Drive past the farm yard and park in the layby on the right at the side of dirt track by a gate. Or keep driving down the track (bumpy with large potholes) to parking spaces by the gate and stile. Please leave gates clear. To find out local tide times, see useful links. Postcode area IV12 5NU.

It is popular to cycle these routes along the hard packed sand when the tide is fully out.

what it's great for

RACES DOWN TO THE WATER'S EDGE AND BACK

BEACH CRICKET WHEN THE TIDE IS OUT

FLYING A KITE

FINE WHITE SAND

HEAVEN FOR DOGS TOO

"Look out for the dolphins and seals who sometimes pop their heads up to see what you're up to"

tips

This beach is exposed to the elements so come prepared to have the wind in your hair or to get surprisingly hot if the sun is out.

WHITENESS BEACH

Furthest distance from Inverness 22km / 13miles

walk options

Beach 600m

Walk 1. 7km

Walk 2. 9km

77

PERFECT BEACHES, NAIRN

Dig, run, comb for shells, swim, paddle, eat ice cream and spot dolphins and seals. Discover these perfect beach days out within an hour from Inverness.

Nairn

Nairn Beach is long and spacious, with fine sand and small dunes to play in. It's also possible to walk or cycle along flat tarmac paths that run directly behind the beach. You'll get views of old Nairn town on one side and the Moray Firth and the Black Isle on the other.

walk 1. Nairn waterfront ✪

1.5km along the front. Standard bike, wheelchair, pram and scooter friendly. Turn right from the car park, continue 500m to the harbour. Cross the metal footbridge over the River Nairn and continue along to the end of the harbour wall. The wilder sandy beach on the right-hand side of the harbour goes for miles and feels untouched and remote.

Turn left from the car park, it is 300m to the first play park with a pirate ship, public toilets, giant paddling pool (open in summer) and tearoom. Keep going along the path to your left and you'll see a putting green/crazy golf and climbing equipment for bigger kids in the trees about 50m off the path. The tarmac path continues for about another 1km.

🍦 **Top ice cream and coffee!** Don't miss **James's on the Putting Green** for coffee and amazing homemade ice cream. Open all year, weekends only in winter, rugs and hot water bottles provided!

walk 2. Nairn to Cawdor ✪

Mostly flat, tarmac/gravel path with very little traffic after Nairn town. This path has narrower sections in the middle that become quite overgrown in the summer so long trousers are recommended! 19km/12 miles return. Standard bike friendly. This route follows a path through farmland alongside the River Nairn. Start from the suggested car park, where there is a route board. Cawdor is a pretty conservation village, with a pub and tearoom. **Cawdor Castle** and grounds is open to visitors (charge) and is linked to the real Macbeth of Shakespeare's play. The woodland outside the castle, behind the village, is also lovely to explore on flat riverside paths.

amenities

Nairn town centre is within walking distance from the beach and has most amenities. The High Street has good fish and chips. There are public toilets by the suggested car park and a public swimming pool and museum (charge).

directions

Inverness 16 miles. From Inverness take the A96 to Aberdeen/Nairn. Drive through Nairn until the first roundabout and take the first left signed to Central Beach and the swimming pool. Take the first right after that and park right down by the beach for free near the bandstand. Postcode IV12 4EA.

Stop and PYO fruit. See the Foodie Adventure on page 92 for a great place near Nairn to pick your own summer fruit.

Great stop off. Brodie Castle & grounds, near Forres. Although **Brodie Castle** and it's splendid grounds are clearly not a beach, a stop here is really recommended. The lawns, paths, woodland and fantastic play park cover a large area and are free to run around. There is a lochan walk, walled garden, café and picnic area too. In spring, the daffodil display here is world renowned. The 16th century castle is **National Trust** (charge to enter the building for non members).

Directions. Inverness 24 miles. Follow the directions to Culbin Forest (page 80), picking up the signs for Brodie Castle at the turn off from the A96. Postcode area IV36 2TE. Small parking charge.

Refreshment tip. By the side of the A96, **Brodie Country Fayre** has delicious cake amongst many other things (free parking).

NAIRNSHIRE & MORAY
Furthest distance from Inverness 58km / 36miles

Alan Davidson, Bridgecommunityproject.org.uk

what it's great for

BBQ IN A BEACHSIDE FOREST

WALK FOR MILES ALONG DESERTED SAND

CYCLE OR SCOOTER ALONG BEACH FRONT PATHS

BEACH COMB FOR SMOOTH STONES AND QUIRKY SHELLS

DISCOVER WHERE NORMANDY BEACH LANDINGS WERE PRACTISED

walk options
Walk 1. 1.5km
Walk 2. 19km

79

PERFECT BEACHES, MORAY

Culbin Forest is a haven for miles of gentle family biking or walking.

enjoy the ride

Culbin Forest & Sands, Moray

The whole of Culbin Forest used to be sand dunes. This pine forest was successfully planted to keep the dunes in place from the 1920's, though some early trees are still buried in up to 5metres of sand! The forest is now a Site of Special Scientific Interest. Scientists are particularly interested in the many different species of spider and butterfly found here. Look for the carpets of happy lichen too.

walk 3. Culbin forest trails ⊗

Mixture of flat trails on forested sand and gravel paths. 1km-8km return. Standard bike and off-road pram friendly. The easy **Hill 99 Trail** (5.7km) leads to a tree top viewing tower you can climb up. Walk a few km further to a deserted stretch of beach on Culbin Sands (be careful of the tide here). Most junctions in the forest are numbered by posts to help you navigate a route from the Forestry Commission Scotland information board maps in the car park.

directions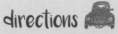

Inverness 26 miles. Take the A96 to Aberdeen. Just before Forres, turn left at Brodie and follow signs to Culbin for 5 miles. Forestry Commission car park (charge) at Wellhill. Postcode area IV36 2TG. **Amenities.** Toilets and picnic tables in car park.

Findhorn Beach, Moray

Findhorn beach and village sit on Findhorn Bay, where seals can often be seen lounging about on the other side of the harbour by Culbin Sands (see above). A short potter from the village, the main beach has huge expanses of sand, perfect pebbles, maram grass covered dunes and pools left behind when the tide is fully out. There is another small bay with some sand by the harbour.

A little bit of history. Findhorn's past includes a thriving fishing and shipbuilding industry. Storms in the 1600s led to the original village being buried by sand dunes. The replacement village was lost to floods in 1701 and the site is still under the sea today. The village site today is the 3rd rebuild!

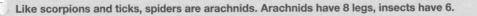

Like scorpions and ticks, spiders are arachnids. Arachnids have 8 legs, insects have 6.

amenities

Findhorn village itself has some great cafés and pubs to sit outside and watch the world go by. The harbour-side **Findhorn Marina** is a go-to spot for local ice cream, food and all things water sports, including a water taxi over to Culbin Sands (charge, seasonal). The interesting **Findhorn Foundation Ecovillage** is open to everyone to walk around or visit the organic café. There are public toilets in the main beach car park (free).

Visit. In the village, the small **Findhorn Heritage Centre and Icehouse** is free to enter. Go in the 150 year old ice chambers, once used to pack salmon bound for London. Seasonal opening. www.findhorn-heritage.co.uk

What's that noise? On the road in to the village, the military have an obvious presence at Kinloss Barracks. If a roaring RAF jet is coming in to land, who can resist the temptation to duck?

walk 4. Findhorn to Burghead

Flat, 16km return. You can walk eastwards all the way along the coast from Findhorn's main beach along Burghead Bay, to Burghead village. It's a stunning part of the Moray Coast Trail. Burghead has the remains of the largest Pictish fort ever built.

directions

Inverness 32 miles. Take the A96 to Aberdeen/Nairn. Pass through Forres. At the Findhorn roundabout take the first exit onto the B9011 signed to Findhorn. After 2 miles you'll reach Kinloss, take the left turn signed to Findhorn and follow it into the village. It is best to head through the village to the ample free parking among the sand dunes behind the main beach (signed as North Beach). Postcode area IV36 3YN.

NAIRNSHIRE & MORAY

Furthest distance from Inverness 58km / 36miles

walk options

Walk 3. 1-8km

Walk 4. 16km

"PERFECT BEACHES, MORAY

Bring a picnic or cook up a barbecue while the children have fun in the play area...

enjoy the view

BE YOURSELF; EVERYONE ELSE IS ALREADY TAKEN. OSCAR WILDE

Roseisle Forest Beach, Moray

Roseisle Forest beach is miles of beautiful sand, Scots pine forest and dunes. During World War 2, the coastal defences of tank traps and pillboxes still lining this beach were used to practice for the Normandy landings. The dunes form part of the largest dune system in the UK. It's a short board walk down to the beach.

amenities

Picnic tables and BBQ areas dot the forest, with a small play park. Seasonal toilets.

directions

Inverness 34 miles. Take the directions to Findhorn (see page 81) but continue through Kinloss onto the B9089. Roseisle Forest beach is signed on the left after 5.4 miles. Forestry Commission Scotland parking charge. Postcode area IV36 2UB.

Cummingston Beach, Moray

Cummingston beach is special for beautiful rock formations, small caves, a stretch of sand and usually being quiet too. An easy path leads down to the beach.

walk 5. Old railway line ⊗

Flat, 3.2km return from Cummingston to Hopeman. **Standard bike, off-road pram.** It's possible to walk or cycle along the old railway line, east from Cummingston beach to Hopeman, a small fishing village with a harbour, places to eat and more beach. East Beach in Hopeman has colourful beach huts, sand and rockpools. This path is part of the continuing Moray Coast Trail.

Keep going on foot (leave bikes in Hopeman) along the coastal cliff path from behind Hopeman's East Beach to the dramatic **Clashach Cove** with it's exciting rock formations. **Take a torch for the cave!** (3.2km return from Hopeman, also known as Cove Bay or Primrose Bay). This area is said to have ancient dinosaur trails, with footprints still evident in the sandstone.

directions

Inverness 36 miles. Follow the directions to Findhorn (above) but continue through Kinloss for 7 miles. Pass Burghead, and continue to Cummingston village initially on the B9089 and then on the B9040. The beach is not signed, so enter Cummingston village, turn onto Seaview road, turn left and follow the road around to the free car park. Postcode area IV30 5XY.

amenities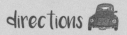

Small play park and public toilets by the car park.

NAIRNSHIRE & MORAY
Furthest distance from Inverness 58km / 36miles

walk options
Walk 5. 3.2km

83

GO LARGE INVERNESS-SHIRE [INCLUDING THE CAIRNGORMS NATIONAL PARK]

As the kids get bigger, so do their expectations of a challenge.

about Go Large

Go Large is a selection of the best bigger routes from local folk who know. Aimed at families with older and more able children, these routes test energy levels and require map and compass skills. The eight walks are all rated red boot and provide a wide variety of terrain including Munro mountain tops, a loch and coastal loop. Start points, a brief route description and the correct Ordnance Survey (OS) map to use to plan your route are provided for each Go Large.

OF ALL THE PATHS YOU TAKE IN LIFE, MAKE SURE A FEW OF THEM ARE DIRT.

adventure safely

Go Large Safety. Go Large routes take on the Highland's true wild side. A map, compass and route planning are required. These routes are recommended here for summer conditions only but always set out prepared for abrupt weather changes. Visibility can become very poor quickly. Check the weather before you set out. www.metoffice.gov.uk and www.mwis.org.uk

walk 1. Meall Fuar-mhonaidh hill, near Drumnadrochit

Gentle approach, then a long, sometimes steep incline on uneven paths to the summit. Allow 4 hours. 9.7km/6 miles return. Meall Fuar-mhonaidh is the highest point on the Northern Loch Ness shoreline, with stunning views in every direction, of the Great Glen and untouched, wild Highland beauty.

Brief description of route. The footpath starts through a gate by a small bridge and pottery, 100m up from the parking area. It's a gentle path through woodland clearly marked to Meall Fuar-mhonaidh. The path turns rocky in places as it joins open heathery hillside and a ridge line. Cross a high deer fence, turn left on the path. Then go steadily up all the way to the top for about 3.2km/2 miles, following a clear path (can get boggy in places). The furthest away cairn sits at 699m (you start walking at around 220m). Return the same way.

Maps. OS Landranger 26 (Inverness and Loch Ness). **OS Explorer 416** (Inverness, Loch Ness and Culloden).

amenities

Drumnadrochit village has all amenities, the central Café 82 is popular with families.

directions to walk 1.

Grid NH 490 238. Inverness 19 miles. Take the A82 towards Fort William. Once through Drumnadrochit, take the right turn signed to Grotaig (Bunloit). Park at the end of this road in a free parking area. Postcode area IV63 6XH.

walk options
Walk 1. 9.7km

GO LARGE INVERNESS-SHIRE
[INCLUDING THE CAIRNGORMS NATIONAL PARK]

walk 2. Loch Affric Circuit, near Cannich ⊗

Good paths with some inclines. Allow 6 hours. 17.7km/11 mile loop. Suitable for mountain bikes. This is a long but gentle route right around Loch Affric, through stunning scenery that gets very remote before heading back through native Caledonian forest. There is incredible wildlife spotting to be done, including deer, otter, golden eagle and capercaillie.

Brief description of route. This route is recommended anticlockwise around Loch Affric for the best views. From the parking area, walk 1.6km towards Affric Lodge, close to the shore. Take the path signed Kintail and Hostel Route which stays quite high above the loch for over 6km. You'll pass wee Loch Coulavie and drop down into the remote upper glen. Turn left, and head back to Loch Affric, crossing a bridge and passing the white cottage of Althnamulloch bothy, and through forest back to the start point.

Maps. Forestry Commission Scotland leaflet, Glen Affric. **scotland.forestry.gov.uk/visit/glen-affric OS Landranger 25** (Glen Carron and Glen Affric) or **Explorer 414** (Glen Shiel and Kintail Forest) and **Explorer 415** (Glen Affric and Glen Moriston).

amenities 🚻WC 🪑

Toilets and picnic tables. No mobile phone reception.

directions to walk 2. 🚗

Grid NH 201 233. Inverness 37 miles. Take the A82 to Drumnadrochit, then the A831 to Cannich. Follow signs to Glen Affric National Nature Reserve. Park in the Forestry Commission Scotland River Affric car park at the end of the road (small charge). Postcode area IV4 7LY.

Fact. A Munro is a peak of 3000ft or 914m, or more. There are 282 in Scotland. **The highest is Ben Nevis, near Fort William.** People make it a lifetime ambition to 'bag' them all. Start now!

The Cairngorms National Park

With 5 out of 6 of the highest mountains in Scotland, the Cairngorms National Park is an obvious place to go for the big stuff. Here are four awesome routes.

Maps. OS Landranger 36 (Grantown and Aviemore). **OS Explorer OL57** (Cairn Gorm & Aviemore).

Tip. For accurate hill weather forecasts in the Cairngorms area visit **mwis.org.uk** and click on Cairngorms National Park and Monadhliath.

enjoy the uphill

THIS IS YOUR EVEREST.
JIM TELFER, LIONS TOUR 1997

walk 3. Meall a Bhuachaille

Meall a Bhuachaille, past the Green Lochan, is a gentle walk on a marked trail, followed by a steep ascent and descent on an unsigned but clear path. **Allow 4 hours. 8km/5 mile loop.** Great views of Loch Morlich and the Cairngorms from a remote hill top.

Brief description of route. This loop starts and ends in the same place as the Ryvoan Trail to the Green Lochan and Ryvoan Bothy. Start by following walk 3 as far as Ryvoan Bothy on the Cairngorm Lochs Adventure on page 39.

Just before the bothy, a path forks left and makes a steep climb to the top of Meall a Bhuachaille (meaning shepherds hill) for about 1.7km, with a cairn at 810m. Head straight over and down the other side. At a path junction, just where the descent evens out on the ridge between Meall a Bhuachaille and another hill (Creagan Gorm) take the path left. This path leads 2km downhill, through Glenmore Forest Park and back to the Glenmore Visitor Centre.

directions to walk 3.

Grid for parking area NH 977 098. For directions see Cairngorm Lochs Adventure, walk 3, page 39.

walk 4. CairnGorm Mountain

Steep ascent to the summit along well used tracks. **Allow 5 hours. 6km/3.7 miles return.** The 6th highest **Munro** at a mighty 1245m, the CairnGorm mountain is very popular with walkers, mountain bikers and skiers.

Brief description of route. The summer walking route to the top is well trodden. From the ski centre car park, take the Windy Ridge Trail; a large, wide track that strikes left from behind the car park phone box, all the way up to the Ptarmigan Restaurant. From the restaurant, the Summit Trail is the most defined and direct way to the top. Retrace your steps.

Route Info. The restaurant and visitor centre in the car park can provide details of the **Windy Ridge Trail** and the **Summit Trail**. Always check the summit weather conditions, it can be VERY windy on top here, even when it feels calm below.

Alternative route. Do one part of the journey to or from the Ptarmigan restaurant on the CairnGorm Funicular Railway, entry charge. **www.cairngormmountain.com**

directions to walk 4.

Grid NH 989 059. Inverness 42 miles. Take the A9 south to Aviemore. From Aviemore, take the B970 and follow signs to the CairnGorm Mountain Railway. Free parking. Buses run from Aviemore to CairnGorm Ski Centre. Postcode area PH22 1RB.

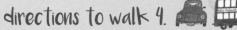

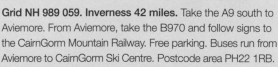

GO LARGE
Furthest distance from Inverness 67km / 42miles

walk options
Walk 2. 17.7km
Walk 3. 8km
Walk 4. 6km

GO LARGE INVERNESS-SHIRE [INCLUDING THE CAIRNGORMS NATIONAL PARK]

Amazing views from the Sgor Gaoith route.

'DIFFICULTIES ARE JUST THINGS TO OVERCOME,
EARNEST SHACKLETON

walk 5. Chalamain Gap

Steady ascent up a good rocky path. The gap itself is boulders. Allow 3 hours. 6km/3.7 miles return.

Brief description of route. Chalamain Gap is a long rocky gully requiring some good rock hopping skills to get through it. It's fun to walk to, have an explore, then return the same way on a clear path. From the start point, cross the river past a reindeer enclosure and shed and continue on a clear path for 3km, taking one right fork after 1.5km. Retrace your steps.

directions to walk 5. 🚗

Grid NH 984 074. Inverness 40 miles. Take the A9 south to Aviemore. From Aviemore, take the B970 and follow signs to the CairnGorm Mountain Railway. The Forestry Commission Scotland car park called The Sugarbowl (parking charge) is on a tight left bend, about 2 miles past Loch Morlich. Postcode area PH22 1RB.

walk 6. Sgor Gaoith from Glen Feshie

Gentle ascent on an excellent path, with final steeper climb to the summit over rougher ground. Map and compass essential. Allow 6 hours. 13km/8 miles return. Sgor Goaith (1118m) is a great Munro to tackle with older kids, with a long steady ascent but dramatic geography, views and very remote.

Brief description of route. From the start point a good path through pines and heather extends 4km on the OS map (ending where it meets the burn Allt a Chrom-alltain). From this point, the ascent is steep but clear, aiming for the flat plateau slightly to the south of the summit, then up. It's stunning but take care, Sgor Goaith is perched right on the edge of a giant sweep of broken crags, where the Feshie plateau falls down to isolated Loch Einich. Retrace your steps.

amenities

See Cairngorm Lochs Adventure page 38.

directions to walk 6. 🚗

Grid NH 853 012. Inverness 40 miles. Take the A9 south. Turn left on to the B9142 signed to Kincraig, continue to Kincraig. From Kincraig, take the B970 past Loch Insh. From Feshiebridge the start point parking area is 2 miles along this road, to the left. There is a visitor's board in the parking area.

GO LARGE
Furthest distance from Inverness 67km / 42miles

walk options
Walk 5. 6km
Walk 6. 13km

89

GO LARGE ROSS-SHIRE

Tackle the closest Munro to Inverness, Ben Wyvis, or walk to a lighthouse around an entire sea peninsula full of wildlife.

bag your first Munro!

'Wyvis' translates as enormous and is the 85th highest Munro. Ben Wyvis is the closest Munro to bag from Inverness, with a good path.

walk 7. Tarbat Ness Peninsular

Gently undulating, a few short climbs and some uneven cliffside paths. Allow 4 hours. 14km/8.7 miles loop. From Portmahomack harbour, this beautiful clockwise coastal walk loops around the entire peninsula, out to Tarbat Ness lighthouse. The path mostly sticks to the coastline, before cutting inland again at the hamlet of Rockfall. It passes a castle and cliffs of sea birds.

For shorter legs. The grassy seaside path at the start is nice to explore from the harbour even if you only intend to go a little way then turn back.

Maps. OS map Landranger 21 (Dornoch and Alness) and **Explorer 438** (Dornoch and Tain)

directions & amenities

Grid NH 915 847. Inverness 41 miles. See Explore a Peninsula on page 70. From the centre of the village, the start of the footpath is signed Tarbat Ness 5km from a free parking area, through a gate, just beyond the harbour.

walk 8. Ben Wyvis

Gentle approach, a long steep ascent, then a gentle incline along a wide ridge (usually windy). Allow 6 hours. 12.9km/8 miles return. Ben Wyvis, which is near Garve stands tall and proud, visible from miles around, often with snow on the top from November to May.

Brief description of route. The start of the path is signed from the car park. It's a gentle uphill path through pines and heather, keeping a burn on your right for about 2km. Even if you don't go to the true summit, it's nice to walk this bit and zig zag up the ascent a little to grab some of the views. The main ascent is steep and quite a puff for over 1.5km, with stone steps, to a first cairn on the south west ridge called An Cabar. The ridge itself is wide and a gentle walk of another 2.8km to the true summit cairn at 3432ft or 1046m. Retrace your steps.

Maps. OS Landranger 20 (Beinn Dearg and Loch Broom). **OS Explorer Map 437** (Ben Wyvis and Strathpeffer).

amenities

See Strathpeffer in Pictish Discoveries on page 60 or Contin in Spectacular Waterfalls on page 64.

directions to walk 8.

Grid NH 410 672. Inverness 30 miles. Take the A9 north. At the Tore roundabout, take the A835 signed to Ullapool. Continue on this road for 4 miles past Garve village. The free Forestry Commission Scotland car park is signed on the right of the road. Postcode area IV23 2PG.

GO LARGE

Furthest distance from Inverness 67km / 42miles

walk options

Walk 7. 14km
Walk 8. 12.9km

91

LOCAL FOODIE ADVENTURE

Discover great local edibles whilst also getting active.

forage for fruit in the wild or pick your own on the farm

Find delicious locally made ice cream, decide on your favourite smelling herb and see how organic cheese is made. Also, discover a tropical glasshouse, exotic animals, a specialist cycle track, great playparks and some more adventure routes while you're at it.

bilberries [blaeberries]

Bilberries are also known as blaeberries in Scotland. From late July through September, woodland and heathery hillsides in the Highlands are brimming with wild bilberries, a mini relative of the blueberry. They are yummy straight from their bush or to take home to put in cakes and crumbles. You can find them in lots of places, often among the heather. In particular, all the **Cairngorm Loch Adventure** routes (page 38), **Pictish Discoveries** on the Cat's Back route (page 60) and **The Nessie Hunter** in Torr Woods (page 26), are good.

walk 1. Torbreck Woods ⊗

The ultimate place for billberries is **Torbreck Woods**, at the start of the South Loch Ness Trail (28 mile walk cycle route to Fort Augustus). Follow the blue squirrel sign posts and pick bilberries to your heart's content (late July to September). The woods are really nice for a walk or bike ride, past a little pond, with fun paths to safely run on ahead.

directions

Inverness 3 miles. Take the B862 to Dores and about 1 mile after the Nessie/Tesco roundabout turn left, signed to Torbreck. Park in the layby 300m along this road. Postcode IV2 6DJ.

Warning. Make sure an adult examines any berry before it is consumed (bilberries above).

wild strawberries

A mini version of their commercial cousin, you can find wild strawberries hiding in hedgerows and thickets of vegetation during the summer. They don't come in big clumps but it's fun to look for them even if you just find a couple to gobble up on the spot. Confirmed sightings of wild strawberries include the **Battlefield Adventure** in hedgerows around the Culloden Viaduct & Clava Cairns (page 20) and **Country Estates** (page 56).

brambles [blackberries]

Brambles grow all over the place in autumn. It would be a challenge to find an adventure that doesn't have any at all! Take some home and put them in an apple crumble, yum! Particularly good spots for brambles include all along the canal and by the river at Docharroch on the **Caledonian Canal Adventure** (page 14), **Country Estates** (page 56), **Iron Age Fort** (page 44), **The Nessie Hunter** on the path behind Dores beach (page 26), and **Treasure Island Explorers** alongside the River Ness (page 8).

LIVE IN THE SUNSHINE SWIM IN THE SEA DRINK THE WILD AIR.

discover a Herb Garden

Inverness Botanic Gardens and Nursery, Inverness. This fantastic place is free and open all year. It has a tropical glasshouse with giant Koi Carp. Can you find the coffee crop? Discover a mock desert full of amazing cacti and beautiful outside gardens with special nature trails set up for kids. Go right to the back of the gardens, through the little gate, and you can find a substantial herb garden and a mini maze. Kids and adults love to smell the different leaves. Buy plants including herbs and trailing cherry tomato plants for mini botanists to nurture and cook with at home (seasonal, all grown here by this community enterprise supporting adults with learning difficulties). There's a café and toilets too.

directions

Inverness 1 mile. Off Bught Road. See the map on page 11 as part of the Treasure Island Explorers.

FOODIE ADVENTURE

Local Food
Our top 10!

LOCAL FOODIE ADVENTURE
Ice cream, cheese and greens.

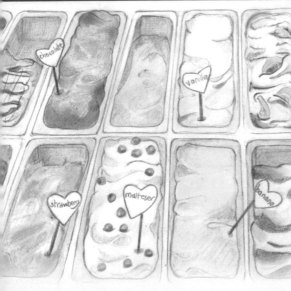

organic cheese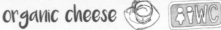

Connage Highland Dairy (or the Cheese Pantry), Ardersier. Discover how cheese is made using traditional organic methods on site and sample more types of cheese than you knew existed. The small café does taster cheese boards, soup, coffee and cake. Open all year.

directions

Inverness 10 miles. Take the A96 to Aberdeen/Nairn. Take the left turn to Ardersier and pick up signs to the Cheese Pantry. Postcode area IV2 7QU

walk 2. Ardersier

Flat, on tarmac and dirt paths. 2km loop. Standard bike, pram and wheelchair friendly. Ardersier Common has picnic tables and an information board showing nature to spot and footpaths, which go along the Moray Firth shoreline. You'll see Fort George Barracks, built after the Battle of Culloden to keep the Jacobites at bay. Pass directly through the village and the common is signed on the left, on the road out to Fort George. The huge village play park is really worth a visit too. Postcode area IV2 7TD

Link a visit to **Ardersier** with the nearby **Wilderness Beach Adventure**, Whiteness on page 76.

'It's never too early, too late or too cold for ice cream'

I scream, you scream, we all scream for ice cream!

There are lots of places to go for great homemade ice cream. We have described how to find some delicious examples under 'Amenities,' in the adventures in **Nairn** and **Findhorn** (page 78), **Cromarty** (page 52), **Inverness City** (page 12) and **Littlemill, Daviot** (page 18).

fruit picking on a farm

Wester Hardmuir Fruit Farm, Nairn.
A great all-weather family venue for fruit picking (open for PYO from late June onwards). It also has a big outdoor play area. The strawberry and raspberry picking is all under cover. There are many other types of fruit to pick as they come into season and a big farm shop too, with local ice cream and cake.

Black Isle Berries, Tore. A farm shop and seasonal fruit picking at Ryefield Farm.

directions

Wester Hardmuir Fruit Farm is 20 miles from Inverness. Take the A96 to Nairn/Aberdeen. The farm is 4 miles east of Nairn, directly off the A96. Postcode area IV12 5QG.

Black Isle Berries is 8 miles from Inverness. Take the A9 north. At the Tore roundabout take the Fortrose exit and it is signed after 300m. Postcode area IV6 7SB.

eat your greens!

Cantry Park, near Croy, has a fantastic café, market garden and aviary. There are free areas to explore all year round. See guinea pigs, small farm animals and an aviary, including a cocky cockatoo that says 'Hello!' Wander the rows of organic vegetables in an outside garden and in a giant greenhouse. The college provides rural skills training for young people with a learning or physical disability.

The indoor **Scottish Exotic Animal Rescue Centre** is on site, a charity housing many different types of rescue arachnids, amphibians, reptiles, rodents and more. There is an entrance fee but is well worth a hands on visit.

directions

Inverness 10 miles. Take the B9006 signed to Croy. 3 miles beyond Culloden Battlefield, just before Croy village, take the right hand turn signed to Brae of Cantray and the Scottish Exotic Animal Rescue Centre. Take this road for just over 0.5 miles. The college is on the left, in a distinctive old stable block. The café, with free parking, is just up past the college. Postcode area IV2 5PP.

Link a **Cantray Park** visit to the **Battlefield Adventure** (page 20) or **Wilderness Beach Adventure** (page 76)

cycle route option ⊗

Just down from Cantray Park is the **Highland Cycle Ability Centre**. Open to all cyclists but specialising in cycling for people with disabilities, the Centre has 1km of smooth, safe, traffic-free tarmac going through peaceful countryside. Bring your own bike or make use of the Centre's wide range of standard and adapted cycles. Phone to book ahead. Located just over the bridge past Cantray Park. Postcode IV12 5XT. www.highlandcycleabilitycentre.com

FOODIE ADVENTURE

Local Food
Our top 10!

93

"" INVERNESS CITY PLAY PARKS

the play parks

Inverness city has an excellent selection of play parks, each a little bit different. As well as the usual swings and slides they all have bigger play equipment that will keep older kids amused too. All have green space to kick a ball about and picnic tables. Here are five favourites.

Bellfield Park

Bellfield Park is a pretty Victorian park with a band stand and a myriad of flowers and shrubs. It is a good stop off during the Treasure Island Explorers walk (see page 8 for directions) and has:

> Six public tennis courts (all year round, book and pay on site, free before midday).

> A putting green and giant outdoor paddling pool open in the summer months.

> Perfect lawns for a picnic. The bandstand is also good shelter from the elements if needed.

> Public toilets and a kiosk selling ice cream, sweets and drinks from Easter to Sept.

> A bike hire company located in the centre with good quality bikes, great for hopping onto the canal cycle paths. **www.tickettoridehighlands.co.uk**

> Limited 2 hour free public parking on Bellfield Park road.

Whin Park

Whin Park can be visited as an extension of Treasure Island Explorers (see page 8 for directions). This big park is right next to the river just up from the Ness Islands, it has:

> A miniature steam railway and a boating lake that are open during school holidays and at weekends from April to September. **www.whinparkinverness.co.uk**

> A kiosk selling snacks and ice cream from Easter to October.

> Public toilets open all year round.

> Plenty of free parking off Bught Road.

96

Walker Park

This tree-lined park is located in the Crown area of Inverness, next to a cricket pitch called Fraser Park on Kingsmills Road (IV2 3LL). It's a 10 minute walk from the city centre. It has:

› Loads of space to play football, fly a kite, just run free.

› No toilet or snack amenities at the park so come prepared!

› Limited 2 hour free parking off Kingsmills Road next to Fraser Park.

Inverness Skateboard/Bike Park & Crazy Golf Park

This community **Skateboard and Bike Park** is free. Bring your own skateboard, BMX or scooter. Some areas are definitely for the skilled only but there are smaller ramps too.

Inverness Crazy Golf next door was refurbished in 2016 and has a small charge. Whin Park and the skateboard park are only 500m apart so could be combined. There is free parking next to the skateboard park.

WHEN LIFE GIVES YOU RAIN, JUMP IN THE PUDDLES.

Inshes District Park

Inshes District Park is out of town by Inshes Retail Park, about 3km east of the city centre.

It has extensive new play equipment including a zip wire and castle with climbing walls and a covered wooden lodge style picnic hut. You can park for free off Stevenson Road (IV2 3DT) and to walk 200m down the landscaped path.

"We don't stop playing because we grow old; we grow old because we stop playing" George Bernard Shaw

CITY PLAY PARKS

Inverness
Top 5 Play parks
97

GAMES FOR ADVENTURERS

A pick of the best games to play and things to do with nature as your backdrop.

wild art

Be an artist anywhere; on the beach, in the woods or in your garden!

Guess who. Pick someone everyone in your group knows; friend, family, cartoon character, the dog etc. Then, create them with whatever you have around you. On the beach this could be rock eyes, seaweed hair, stick teeth or crab shell ears. In a wood, you could use moss, twigs, lichen etc. Everyone makes one, then you each have a guess at who has been created.

Make a modern masterpiece. Make a piece of art out of what you find lying about in the open. You can use anything; stones, rubbish, your scarf, etchings onto rock, grass, twigs. Create a beautiful abstract concept all of your own or a sheep, a landscape, whatever grabs your imagination. Get someone to judge the winner (making sure there are lots of winner categories of course).

Cloud play. We have plenty of clouds, so take a rest and all lie on your backs alongside each other. Be quiet for one minute. Make people's faces, animals and random objects out of the clouds. It's amazing what you'll see in what was just a grey blob a few minutes ago. How many different things can people make out of the same cloud?

Make a nature walk bracelet. Take some masking tape or parcel tape out with you. Wrap it around wrists so the sticky side is on the outside. Try to cover as much of the tape as possible with natural objects found along the way (not really a wet weather one this!).

Rubbings. Take white paper and colour crayons on your adventure. Find trees with interesting bark and use the side of the crayon to rub hard and make a pattern emerge on the paper. Make a rubbing of anything, coins and leaves laid on a firm surface are good. Take it all home, cut out the patterns and make a big collage.

EVERY CHILD IS AN ARTIST. THE PROBLEM IS STAYING AN ARTIST AS AN ADULT. PABLO PICASSO

GAMES

keep them moving

Sometimes even adventurers say 'No more!' These games should perk everyone up a bit.

Go get. This game is best played with a few small rewards to hand. Whilst walking, an adult says for example, 'Go get something blue.' Everyone runs off to find something blue and the first person back to the adult with an item gets a sweet (or a point). Always keep walking slowly onwards and suddenly you've passed that last mile! It can get quite competitive and to make it fair for smaller ones, some imaginative tweaking of what needs to be fetched may be required (the small person may be the only person wearing pink spots for example).

Jockeys. Pick a big stick. He is now your horse, give him a name and a handful of grass to eat. Climb on your horse. He's frisky so steady him. Line up with the other horses and jockeys and say 'Go!' This is a steeplechase so detour to find jumps to gain points! Stopping for a second to let your horse rest is also OK. If you prefer a motorbike to a horse, choose a colour, rev up and go but be sure to stop to refuel!

Music. It's amazing how a song can pick up even the grumbliest of walkers. For younger kids, the Grand Old Duke of York, stepping in time, is magic! Older kids might want to play guess the lyrics or guess the theme tune to someone who can whistle or hum.

Stuck in the mud. This game is like tig. One person is it and chases the others. When caught, that person has to stop and stand in a star shape. Someone crawls between their legs to free them. **Make it harder.** If the stuck person can count to 5 before being rescued, they must go down to their knees for a harder rescue!

Scavenger hunt. Get ready to find a:

round leaf	☐	pine cone	☐
very straight stick	☐	piece of moss	☐
leaf with 5 points	☐	seed or nut	☐
big blackberry	☐	pine needle	☐
white stone	☐	something yellow	☐

Handstands and cartwheels. These never fail to amuse the kids especially when an adult thinks they can still cartwheel like a 10 year old.

GAMES FOR ADVENTURERS

'In play, children learn how to learn.' O.Fred Donaldson

Sticks and Stones

Once the sword fights are over, here's some more things to do with those sticks. And stones. And trees.

Bombs away! On a stone beach, build a tower of stones on a bigger rock and try to knock it over by taking turns to throw one stone each at a time. Another version is to work as a team to throw stones at a floating log or stick to see how far out you can move it.

Learn to skim stones. An essential life skill to have! Choose three stones each and have a competition to see who can get the highest total of skims from three throws.

Hug a tree. One person closes or covers their eyes. The other person takes them by the arm leading them carefully to a tree to let them hug it and get to know it for a few seconds. They then take them back to the start point (add in a few diversions or spin them around a bit). The tree hugger can then open their eyes and has to work out which tree they were hugging by testing each one. Can the hugger guess what species of tree it was?

Journey stick. Take one decent sized stick and some wool or small elastic bands. Along the walk, help the kids tie any objects they find onto the stick. By the end you have a stick that tells the story of your walk.

Pooh sticks. Pick a racing stick or twig each. Stand on the side of the bridge with the water flowing towards you. Everyone drop their stick after the count of 3 and run to the other side of the bridge to see who's comes in first.

Tree gaze. Lie under a tree and look up at the patterns made by the branches and leaves. Close your eyes, listen to the tree noises. Imagine what lives in your tree, real or make believe. Talk about how old you think it is and what it may have seen happen in this spot over the years.

Or, draw over a few of the lines in the palm of your hand and then try to find 'your' tree – a tree that has a similar pattern of branches to your palm. Sit by it for a little while.

Rockpools. Get nose to water and explore the magical hidden world of rockpools.

Climb a tree. Simple as that!

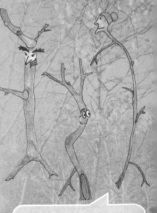

Try drawing your own stickpeople. Where will they have adventures?

100

Let your imagination run wild!

Use those amazing imaginations and time will melt away.

Linking to a story. Link the walk or surroundings to a favourite story or theme and see imaginations run wild. Can you find Peter Rabbit's burrow? Gruffalo footprints? The troll's bridge? The Stick Man family tree? A witch's cavern? A dragon lair? A crocodile tooth? A dinosaur egg? A fairy door in the tree? Can you find things round about you to improve the houses for them?

Build a story. One person starts by saying 'Once upon a time there was a girl/boy called… (pick the name of someone in the group).' Each person in the group has to add a sentence or two in turn using something they can see around them (dog, stream, red scarf), to build up a usually very funny story about what happens to that person. It can keep going as long as you like!

Set up camp. Pick a tree trunk or low hanging horizontal branch and lean long sticks against it to form a shelter. It doesn't matter if it's quite basic! If you're on the beach, two big sticks in the ground and a picnic blanket over the top with stones to hold out the sides makes a fun hideout for smaller kids. Send the hunters off to find some food. Find some log or stone seats. Then build a pretend campfire to roast your pretend wild boar on (or a real one with marshmallows if it is safe and an adult is confident to do so!).

Water crossing. The puddle or stream is a giant sea full of sharks and crocs. Find things to use as stepping stones to get across it. Don't let your toes slip in… Or, capture water by damming up a stream. Then let it all escape again. Where will your water end up? Or, just have a splash about!

A bugs life. Gently lift a big stone or old fallen branch. Peer in and find some creatures living there. Who's who in this amazing little mini world? Is everyone friends? What do they eat for lunch? Where do they sleep at night and are they scared of the dark?

Build your perfect house. Sandcastle building competition!

WHY, SOMETIMES I'VE BELIEVED MORE THAN SIX IMPOSSIBLE THINGS BEFORE BREAKFAST. ALICE THROUGH THE LOOKING GLASS

GAMES

These pages are to help you remember your adventures forever.

"DOODLE OR SKETCH"

"WRITE OR STICK YOUR PICTURES HERE →

Insects you might have seen along the way.

Bug hunt. How many can you find?

spider	☐	honey bee	☐
blue butterfly	☐	pond skater	☐
ladybird	☐	moth	☐
damselfly	☐	Red Admiral	☐
dragonfly	☐	beetle	☐

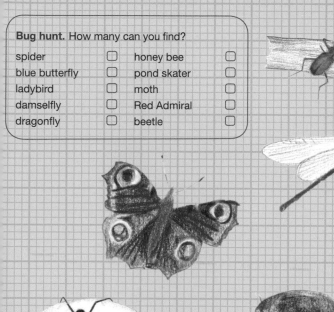

Draw your favourite bug here.

My Notes!

EXPECT THE UNEXPECTED, AND WHENEVER POSSIBLE, BE THE UNEXPECTED. LYNDA BARRY

103

DOODLE OR SKETCH

enjoy the view

Draw your favourite landscape or view:
mountains, wooland, loch or sea.

WRITE OR STICK YOUR PICTURES HERE →

Why not design your own adventure page?

Please tell us about it. www.weeadventurescotland.co.uk

Black Isle Bicycles / Ewen Weatherspoon

"ENJOY YOUR ADVENTURES!"

Forestry Commission Scotland
Coimisean na Coilltearachd Alba

TESCO Bags of Help